SCROLL SAW
Woodcrafting
MAGIC

by Joanne Lockwood

Three Bears Workshop

CHAPEL Fox Chapel Publishing
Box 7948
Lancaster, PA 17604

Scroll Saw Woodcrafting Magic!
Copyright 1993, Fox Chapel Publishing.

Library of Congress Cataloging - in - Publication Data
Lockwood, Joanne
    Scroll Saw Woodcrafting Magic! / by Joanne Lockwood.
    p. cm.
    Includes index
    ISBN# 1-56523-024-8
    1. Jig saws.   2. Woodwork.   I. Title
    TT186.L36 1992
    684'.083—dc20   92-37405
                CIP

Cover and interior photography: *Bob Pollett, VMI Productions, Leola, PA*
Cover design & interior typography: *Mouse Pad Studios, Lancaster, PA*

The patterns for collapsible baskets that appear in this book are copyrighted by the Berry Basket. Used by permission. The color paint chart is copyright Delta/Shiva Paints. Used by permission.

To order your copy of this book, send check or money order for cover price plus $2.50 to:

Fox Chapel Publishing
Box 7948 J
Lancaster PA 17604

Try your favorite book supplier first!

92 93 94 95 1 2 3 4 5
Manufactured in the United States of America

TABLE OF CONTENTS

Dedication:

When I was a young girl, I used to love watching my Dad out in his tiny little garage working on his ShopSmith. I marveled as he would switch from one tool to another, cutting, turning, sawing, or sanding, until he came up with a completed project. The little smirk on his face when he would finally take it in and show it to my Mother - he was so proud.

I can't help but think how pleased he would be to see what his youngest daughter ended up doing for a living. I know if he were here, he would be right out there with me, (telling me what to do of course), and marveling at the same time at how far the tool industry has advanced. (He had never even heard of a scroll saw!)

There is never a time when I am in my shop that "Daddy" is not in my thoughts

I lovingly dedicate this book to his memory.

Acknowledgments

With love and special thanks to:

My scroll saw students for their faith in my ability to instruct them in the proper use of the scroll saw.

My old Tuesday night painting pals, Donna, Darlene, Marilyn and "Bob" - for their support and laughter when I needed it the most.

A very special thanks to Marilyn Nishikawa for her wonderful humor and for the ability she has to convince me that I am capable of conjuring up just about anything ! Thanks Marilyn - you are a very special friend.

Joanne Lockwood

Hugs to my tiny Wednesday night tole painting class, Newell, Pat and John, for putting up with me when I appeared to have suffered from temporary "loss of brain function", from being on work overload. Thanks for your patience.

A very large thank you to Newell Hubbard for cutting many of the fretwork patterns in this book for me. Newell is a Search and Rescue volunteer, and enjoys scroll sawing on his days off, when he gets them. He and his wife Pat, have become very dear friends as well as students. Thank you Newell.

Most of all my husband Max, who has taken over most of my duties in the house, as well as all of them in the woodshop while I have been busy trying to meet the deadline for this book. I can never thank him enough!

This book would never had taken place if it weren't for Fox Chapel Publishing, and I want to thank them for their faith in me.

Introduction

In my first book, "Learning to use your Scroll Saw" I taught a particular technique with every project offered. In this book I will take you into the wood shop, give you specific instructions to prepare, cut, sand and assemble each project, and then take you into the painting studio where you will get specific painting instructions as well.

Many of the painted pieces will be very basic, with little shading so the budding artist will not be intimidated.

You will find you do not have to be an artist to paint a piece. By following the step by step instructions, the end result will be very pleasing to the eye, and should give the beginner a wonderful sense of accomplishment.

REMEMBER : practice really does make perfect. Do not be harsh with yourself if you do not produce a perfect product the first time out. I think if you can remember back in time, (a very long time for some of us) that you were pretty wobbly when you took your first step, but you sure didn't give up. You wanted to
get somewhere so you just kept falling down and get-ting up until you had mastered walking. Well, the same thing applies to all art forms. Practice until you quit "falling down".

We are going to cover a few of the very basics in scroll saw-ing before we start on a project, so sit down, get comfortable, and read on.

Oh, yes I know you're going to skip right on to the projects. Everyone tries that. Eventually you will return and read the first chapter or two though when things are not going quite right, and the saw is not performing properly, (or could it be you?) You'll be back to read the rest of the "boring" informa-tion. Go ahead ... See you later!

A Note From the Author

While it is not my intention to give free advertisement to any one product or manufacturer, I feel it a service to pass on the names of those I have had good experience with, and have found to be superior.

I'm sure you have all heard the expression "experience is the best teacher". Well, I've experienced a lot of machinery in the last 10 years, and wasted a lot of money in the process. I have also tried a lot of different painting supplies over the years, and have my good old standbys in that department also. So when I find something dependable and or superior, I like to pass it on.

However, this does not mean you should take my word as gospel, and go right out and by the products I use and recommend. Check out any product you are about to spend your hard-earned money on before you buy. Get some "hands on" experience if at all possible. The products I recommend at least give you a place to start looking.

Experiment for yourself on the many different brands on the market. Chances are you will find the ones I recommend to be the best. But when you decide on them, it will be due to your own personal knowledge and experience - not because some one else told you that they were good!

Chapter 1

You and Your Choice of a Scroll Saw

You and Your Choice of a Scroll Saw

There are many brands of scroll saws on the market today. Some are good, some not so good. It is very hard, unless you really know machinery, to know which one to buy and trial and error is a bit expensive for the average person. Here are a few pointers before you start shopping for your first saw (or shopping for an upgrade to the one you already have).

What type of material will you be working with? Know what size stock you want to be able to saw through. Know how intricate you want to cut, and on what materials other than wood you will be cutting (i.e. glass, metal, plastic paper, cloth etc.).

When you are ready to buy or at least look into purchasing a saw, take the material you want to cut with you, and ask the sales person to allow you to cut it. If you are refused with the comment - " sorry but our insurance will not allow customers to cut on the machinery" - ask the salesperson to cut it for you.

If the response is a "Gee, I know it will cut, but I just really am not familiar with the saw and George is out to lunch" routine, chances are the saw you are looking at will not cut what you want it to cut. My suggestion is to go somewhere that allows you or at least the salesman to cut actual test pieces.

When you do find a salesperson who is willing to cut , find out the following.

a. How thick will the machine cut (the maximum is $2\,^5/_8''$)

b. How big a piece of stock can you turn around and still clear the throat with it. This will be the depth of the throat. Your turning ratio is from the blade to the back of the arm.

c. How difficult is it to insert a blade? Not just slip a pre-clamped blade into the machine, but to take a brand new blade, install the blade clamps and install the blade into the machine.

This is probably the biggest drawback to any saw. If the blade change takes three hands I would shy away from that machine (unless you have three hands).

d. Find out how tightly you can make turns without the blade breaking, and see to it that they install a small blade (size #3). Many machines can turn wonderfully with a large blade, but will not carry a small one without breaking it.

e. Will the saw follow a curved line? It does take a little practice. Most of the pin type blades have a lot of difficulty following a curve.

f. Does the upper arm stop when the blade breaks? This is a great safety feature. Don't take anyone else's word for it...ask them to remove a blade and turn the machine on. If the upper arm is stationary it means it stops when the blade breaks. If it continues to move up and down, it is not. It is that simple.

g. What kind of noise does it make in general ? What kind of racket does it make when the blade does break? Some of them will scare you out of a years growth!

h. Does the saw vibrate badly?

There are so many thing to look for aren't there? When you finally find the saw you think is right for you, wait a minute before you sign on the dotted line... Ask a few more questions.

a. How long is the warranty, and what does it cover? It would stand to reason the longer the warranty, the longer the machine is going to run trouble free. Companies usually do not offer a long warranty if they know the machine isn't built to last a long time.

b. Where do you take it for repairs?

c. Availability and cost of replacement parts and supplies.

d. Last but not least- how long has the company been around ? If it has been around a long time, it has developed some sort of reputation. Check it out with your woodworking friends!

Remember, it is your hard earned money you are spending. If the salespeople are offended because you ask "too many questions", there has to be a reason for it.

If you are a serious sawyer and have purchased a saw that you are not happy with, and are confident that it is not anything you are doing wrong - take it up with the company. Be reasonable. If you have had your saw for a long while, and have never complained to the company about it, it's a bit unlikely they will do a lot at this late date (you can try, but be fair, and make sure it is a legitimate complaint). There is nothing worse than a customer calling a company after three years and saying - " I want my money back, this thing has never worked right!" Having never complained in those three years to the company, there is nothing they are going to do for you. Take your losses and upgrade to a top of the line saw.

95% of the students taking my seminars who bring in inferior saws had almost given up on their dream of becoming good on the saw. They felt they just didn't have what it takes. When they were transferred to my saw, - because theirs was not able to do the class projects - they improved dramatically! So don't be discouraged if you cannot perform as you would like on your saw. Chances are it is the saw that is the culprit.

It is no secret that I prefer the German - made Hegner scroll saw for my own personal use as well as for teaching students. I enjoy the quiet operation, the precision, and most of all the absolute dependability.

There is a little scroll saw on the market however that has recently caught my eye. It has been brought into my classroom on several occasions, and has performed very well.

It is the PennState scroll saw. While I normally would never recommend anything made in Taiwan, I have found this saw to be the best in its price range. (under $200.00).

There are many other saws made in many different places available to choose from. These are the two that I personally consider to excel in their individual price range.

This information is supplied to you only as a guideline. See source pages for more information on manufacturers.

While I may recommend these pieces of equipment, I can not personally guarantee them.

Let's do a quick overview of the essential facts about scroll saws.

Scroll saws are for doing precise work on an infinite variety of materials. They will saw the thinnest of veneers to produce incredible inlays, but at the same time can cut up to 2″ thick stock as well. (One machine will even cut up to 2 ⅝″).

They are certainly not meant to create full size furniture, but can create wonderful miniature versions.

They are not for ripping a 2x4 , but with the proper blade and saw, you could do it very slowly. Believe me - you don't want to! If you want to cut thick wood fast, buy a band saw! Scroll saws are not fast, but you can do so many wonderful things with them. With the right saw you can cut metal, glass, plastic or even 100 sheets of paper at one time for that fancy paper cutting. Quilters can pile squares of quilt fabric 2″ deep and cut diamond shapes out 50 and 60 at a time, - the possibilities are almost endless.

Planning your purchase - first think about what you want to use your scroll saw for, and plan your machinery purchase accordingly.

Here is one example of thinking through your purchase completely in advance. If you travel to very many craft shows, you need to think of portability. You will need a sturdy light weight machine that is not going to fall apart or need to be taken apart all the time to transport. You need a three - legged stand that will find its own level on any ground. The four-legged versions either have to be leveled every time you move the machine, or they will wobble badly. You will prefer a welded stand over a bolted one, as bolts come loose with vibration and the constant traveling will loosen up a bolted stand very easily.

Speeds: There are three types of saws on the market:

Constant speed versions - are exactly that. They will always and only operate at one speed.

Multiple speed versions - usually have two or more speeds and are usually changed by moving a belt manually or by shifting a lever from one pulley to another. This is time-consuming and can be very awkward.

Variable speed versions - here you have infinite speed control that can be adjusted anywhere you like from the top speed of the machine to the lowest speed by turning a dial. I personally prefer this type, as I find them to be quieter, and have less vibration that the other two. This version is an absolute must for cutting glass.

Type of mechanisms: There are two basic types of scroll saws available today. Single "C" arm saws, and dual-arm saws. Let me briefly explain the differences, as they are important.

In the "C" arm saws, the upper and lower arms are formed out of a single piece of metal, and therefore must move together. To demonstrate this, hold your hand in front of you and look at it from the side. Now form a "C" with your fingers and thumb. Bend your wrist up and down. This is the motion you will get with a single arm saw. It is impossible to expect a vertical cut with this type of saw.

A dual arm saw has totally separate upper and lower arms. The more parallel they are of course the better, as only a true parallel arm can produce a consistently square cut. Beware that not all saws advertising parallel arms provide the benefit you expect. To check this, turn the motor off, and move the saw arms up and down while viewing the movement of the blade from the side. The more the blade moves from vertical during the stroke, the less vertical your cuts are likely to be.

Another consideration is the safety feature that stops the upper arm when a blade breaks. No "C" arm saw offers this, and only some dual arm saws do. Be sure and check for this as well.

You will find in the chart following information that will help you better understand what each individual may or may not need in a scroll saw. This chart covers most applications for the average woodcrafter.

Scroll Saw Reference Chart

Task	What to look for	Recommendation
Fretwork	Ability to remove blade easily. More than one speed Ability to insert blade after it has been threaded through wood	Quick clamp release Variable speed Slotted table.
Veneer work	More than one speed Ability to hold tiny blades Low vibration Tiltable table (left or right)	Variable speed Research this!. Research ! Either
Cutting thick stock	Saw that cuts perpendicular Thickest cutting depth possible	Parallel arm $2\,\tfrac{5}{8}''$ is max.
Children's use	SAFETY EQUIPMENT! Upper arm must stop when blade breaks Upper blade clamp must not fly out when blade breaks You must have a blade guard	RESEARCH!
Commercial use	Durability. Good reputation	Long warranty Ask questions!
Show circuits	Portability Easily assembled Easy to level	Sturdy but light weight. Welded stand 3 legged stand
Glass cutting	Variable speed only Drip system available? Very low vibration Ability to carry diamond blades	Research!
Metal Cutting	Variable speed only Ability to carry jewelers blades	Check this out!

*The quick clamp release (source page) allows you to release the top of the blade with out using any tools at all. It has finger tip control. This does not release tension. While there are some machines that do have a quick release tension lever or knob, unless the throat of the machine is over 20″, I find this feature quite useless, and even then I still prefer my infinite tensioning control.
(Some machines do offer both).

It is just as easy for me to release the tension at the rear of the machine. The exception to this of course would be if the operator of the machine is rather small and has difficulty reaching to the rear of the machine. Then it would be worth it's weight in gold!

The VS-15 scroll saw from Penn State Industries.

The Excalibur 24 scroll saw from SEYCO Sales—24″ variable speed.

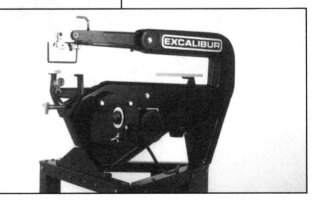

Hegner Scroll Saws

Multimax 14E. A basic entry-level model with a 14″ throat.

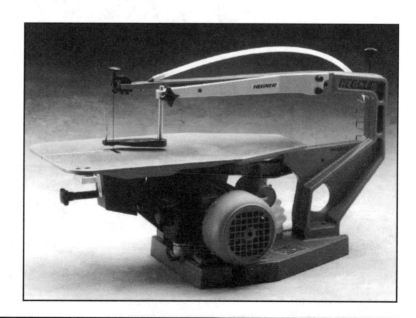

Multimax 18V. A variable speed model with an 18″ throat and a thickmess capacity of 2 ⅝″.

Multimax 25V. A top of the line model with a giant throat depth of 25″ A heavy duty saw with a variety of speed and stroke settings.

Multimax 22V. A new 22″ model with a dual tensioning system.

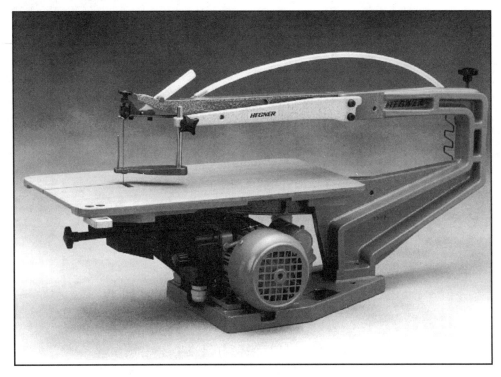

Chapter 2

Scroll Saw Basics

SCROLL SAW BASICS

There are several aspects of using the saw that should be covered before you begin actual hands on operation. I will cover them as briefly as possible in this chapter. Learn these well, they are essential to safe and successful sawing.

Blade installation and tensioning:

Install your blade according to your manufacturers instructions, making sure the teeth are pointed down and towards you when installed.

While this may sound a little too simple to even bother with, an improperly installed blade is not uncommon in my seminars. At least two students in every seminar I have taught will at some time or another install the blade upside down. This is quite easy on some of the small blades we use, as the teeth are very difficult to see.

If you have a blade installed backwards (teeth pointing to back of machine) it is very easy to tell, as the blade simply will not cut anything (except Styrofoam)! On the other hand if you have a blade installed upside down (teeth pointing up), one of several things can happen.

1. The wood will lift up off the table to excess especially on turns.

2. You will have a difficult time following a line

3. You may see a great deal of top chipout.

4. Sawdust will build up on the cutting line (unless you have a very good sawdust blower)

5. An exception occurs when you are using a very small (#3 or smaller) blade you will be able to cut quite well, without really noticing much of anything except a little fuzz on the cutting line. It may even feel as if the blade is dull.

Tensioning your machine:

Use your manufacturers recommended tensioning to begin with. Each machine has a particular feel of it's own when it comes to proper tensioning.

On the projects in this book, unless otherwise stated, "normal" tensioning will be as follows:

Loosen the tension completely, now turn the tension knob until you feel resistance. Turn it an additional 3/4 of a turn from that point. This is normal on all of my machines.

At this point your blade should be taut enough to enable you to follow a line easily, but no so tight that the blade breaks every two minutes! If the blade seems too wishy washy, and sways from side to side on the turns, it probably needs a little more tension.

If it is almost impossible to hold a straight line, it again needs more tensioning. It will not take you a great deal of time to figure this out for yourself.

On machines with a greater depth than 18″ in the throat, the tensioning will need to be somewhat more, up to 1½ turns.

On very small blades - #3 or under - you will need to decrease the tensioning on some machines or the blade will break.

On very large blades - #9 or above - you may want to increase your tensioning.

Increase tensioning whenever you are cutting on 2″ stock. If you are not getting a good straight up and down cut consider the possibility that too little tensioning is the cause.

Don't be afraid to experiment with that little knob. If your blades break rapidly or they slip out of the clamps, it could be too much tension.

If you see more than one blade, it could be too little tension. It should be noted that this "double" blade effect will always be there on a "C" arm saw even if your tensioning is perfect.

Squaring the saw table:

On some projects, especially projects such as the 3-dimensional picture pieces elsewhere in the book, it is imperative your table is square to the blade. If it is not, your cut will not be perpendicular. This could present quite a problem on a jig saw puzzle, as the pieces would only go in one way, and that may very well be from the bottom!.

How to square the table:

Lift the upper arm as high as it will go with your hand. Hold a 2″ metal square along side the blade. **(see photo # 1)** If the table is square the blade will be flush up against the square, top to bottom. If it is not you will see a space between the blade and the square. To correct this problem look under the table for the knob that releases your protractor. That's the little piece of metal with the numbers on it under the table **(see photo #2)** Unloosen this and tilt your table in whatever direction necessary to line the blade up with the square. **(see photo # 3)** Hold it steady while you tighten it back up.

If you prefer not to invest in a metal square, get a piece of 2″ wood and make a shallow cut into it. .Now place the wood behind the blade and see if the cut lines up with the blade. **(Photo #4)** If it does not, follow the steps above until the blade will slip into the cut you made without moving the wood back and forth. While a metal square is more accurate, and perhaps a bit simpler to use, the wood will suffice.

Now the bad news. Some types of machines will never give you a nice perpendicular cut no matter what you do. If you have the disadvantage of having one of those, you will just have to work around it.

(Try feeding your wood square into the blade and it will help keep it straight.)

Speed:

Unless otherwise noted full speed will be used on all of these projects. That should make those of you who do not have a variable speed or multiple speed machine very happy.

Photo 1 *This machine is badly off square, Notice that the blade is further away from the square's edge than the bottom.*

Photo 2 *Adjusting protractor showing 0-45 angles. Loosen knob to release.*

While a variable speed is not necessary unless you wish to do metal or glass cutting, I prefer one, as they appear to run quieter than the single or multi-speed machines. They also appear to cut a little slower than the single speed however.

Changing the Blades

When is it necessary to change the blade? Good question! And there's no obvious answer except the one my oldest granddaughter gave one day at a show. "When it breaks!". While that of course is true, there are other times it becomes necessary to chance the blade as well.

Experience will eventually dictate when to change the blade, but in the meantime a few pointers to help you out:

1. The wood will become difficult to "feed" into the blade, feeling as if it is stuck on something.

2. Your cut will start to look choppy and it will be necessary to sand.

3. It may become impossible to follow a line.

4. The wood may burn.

If you have installed a new blade and any of the above are happening, it could be the grain of the wood that is causing the problem.

Note: When choosing your wood, try and find a close grained wood. This is especially true of pine, as the further apart the grain is the more problem you will have getting a nice cut.

See the wood and materials chapter and accompanying chart elsewhere in this book.

Making multiple cuts - (Stack-cutting)

When you are going to cut more than one of an item you will want to stack the wood and cut several at a time depending on the thickness of the original piece.

To do this, cut your wood to size, apply the pattern, and then tape masking tape all the way around the edge. This is sufficient to hold the pieces together while you cut them. You can

Photo 3   *After adjusting protractor. Blade lines up evenly with square.*

Photo 4   *A square job. Shallow cut lines up with blade.*

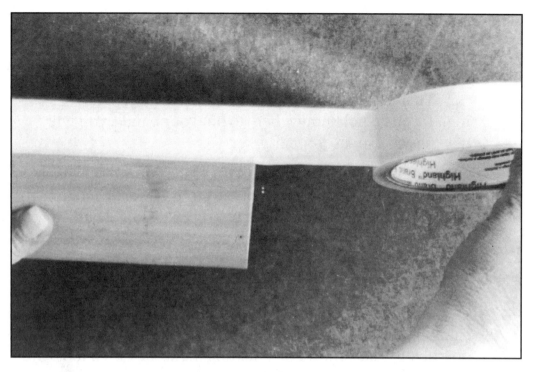

Photo 5   *Taping together stacked wood in preparation for making multiple cuts.*

Photo 6   *Basic hand positioning - always have a hand on each side of the blade.*

stack as high as your saw will allow, however I prefer cutting thinner stacks in the hardwoods.

Hand Positioning

This could very well be the most important phase of sawing!. If you do not know where to put your hands, you will never be able to saw properly.

Place a hand on each side of the blade **(photo # 6)** in a position as close to the center of the piece as is safe. Holding the wood way out at the edge is not only cumbersome, but dangerous. You are off balance, and this makes turning the wood extremely difficult. It also has a tendency to make the wood chatter on the table.

Hold your hands as flat as possible. This will keep the lift to a minimum. You do not have to white knuckle the hold down on a quality machine, in fact holding the wood down too tightly only hinders the turning, and tires you out.

Never have your whole hand and wrist in front of the blade! You are putting yourself in a very dangerous position, and you are off balance again.

Keep your shoulders square to the table at all times. If you can remember to do this you will never have your hands crossed over in front of the blade.

When you are sawing and begin a turn, rather than lifting your hands off the wood to reposition them, try sliding them around over the wood as you guide it. I seldom ever remove my hands from the wood surface. It is best to slide them around as you make each turn - keeping equal pressure on each side of the wood. This minimizes the tendency of the blade to lift up the piece you are working on.

Making tight turns

When maneuvering a tight turn remember to always keep the motor running! This is sometimes a very difficult thing to remember for people who use a sewing machine. They are used to stopping the machine when they turn the material. When you do that you are turning the blade. When the motor is started again, the blade is jammed and lifts the wood off the table - mak-

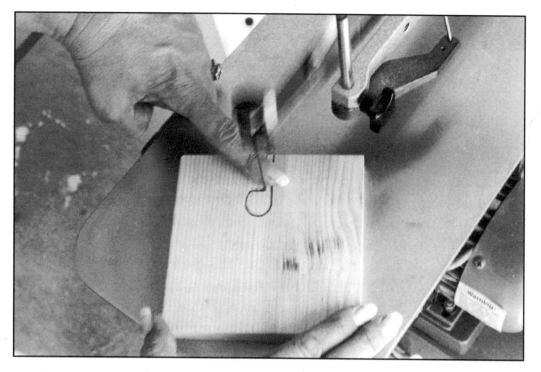

Photo 7   *Pivot point - essential for making tight, crisp turning cuts.*

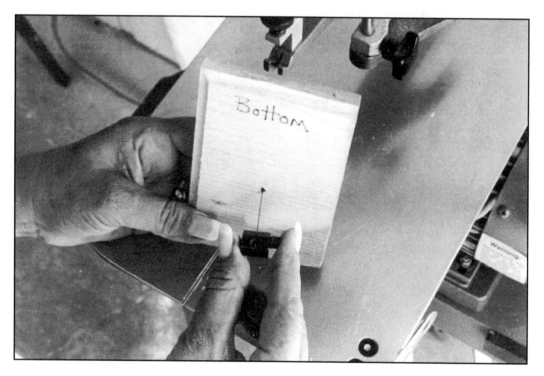

Photo 8   *Inserting the top of blade through pre-drilled hole from the bottom in preparation for making inside cuts.*

ing an awful racket! To execute a smooth turn, position your hands, one on each side of the wood. As you begin your turn, slowly slide your hands on the wood, while you turn. When doing a very tight turn, you will position one finger to the left or right of the blade about an inch away **(photo #7)** holding it there as a pivot point while you turn your wood with the other hand.

You should listen to the machine while maneuvering 90 degree turns. Try this. Make a 2″ cut into the wood, and listen to the cutting noise the saw blade is making. When you get ready to make a sharp turn, stop pushing the wood, put your finger about and inch away from the blade, and pivot around until you have reached the 90 degree point and begin to saw again. Now do this again and listen to the blade cutting into the wood while you cut, listen while you pivot. You should not hear any cutting noise at all when making a sharp turn! Line the saw up with the next line and listen again as you start cutting. If you will train your ear to listen, you will always have very sharply defined corners.

Fretwork and inside cuts

Inside cuts are those which require the pre-drilling of a hole to insert the blade through so that you do not have to cut into the piece from the outside edge. It is a simple but time-consuming technique.

Apply your pattern and pre-drill a hole just big enough for the blade you are using to fit through for every section of wood that is to be removed. Remove the blade from the upper blade clamp, insert it the blade through the hole from the underside of the wood, and re-insert the blade in the upper blade clamp **(Photo # 8)**. Tension the machine and cut the section to be removed out. When finished, release the tension on the machine, remove the top of the blade from the clamp, slip the blade out of the wood, and insert it into the next hole. Re-attach the blade into the blade holder **(Photo #9)**, tension the machine and repeat the process all over again until all sections have been cut out.

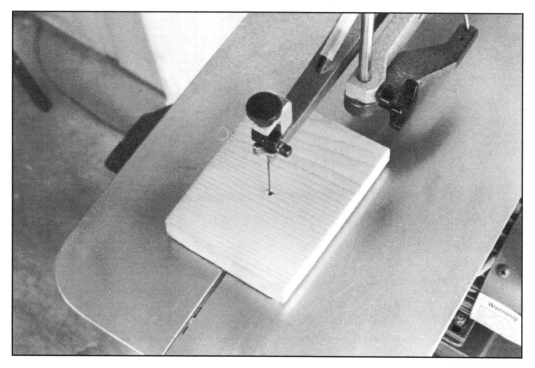

Photo 9   *Blade re-attached to upper clamp-ready to saw*

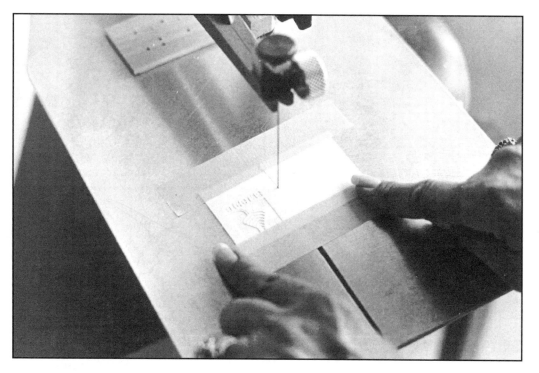

Photo 10   *Temporary overlay for cutting small items. Cut into card and tape in place. Note Quik-clamp attached to upper clamp.*

Where to drill the hole and where to start the cut.

If you are removing a large section of wood, it really doesn't make a great deal of difference where you drill the hole, but if you are removing a very tiny section not much bigger than the blade itself, it is important to choose your drilling place carefully. I always try to drill the start hole in a corner or tight curve rather than on a straight line as it will show less. You will notice this on the 3-D scenes in the projects.

I have drawn a sketch below and marked the good spots to drill as well as where to start your cutting to help you better understand this important skill.

CORRECT   WRONG

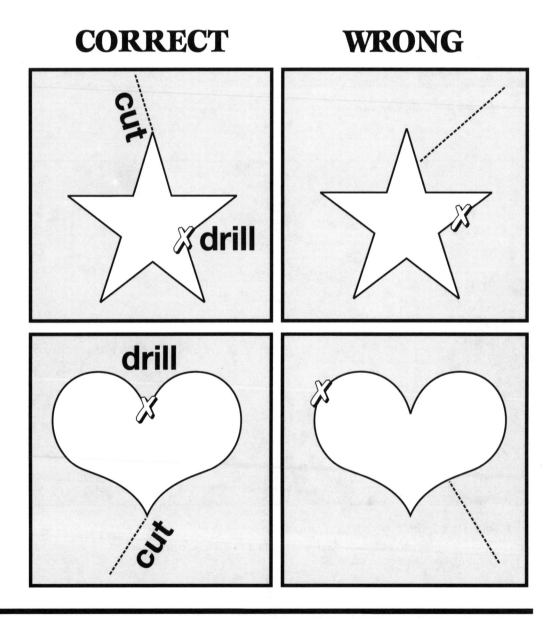

Always start your cutting the same way. Pick a corner if possible, so that when you come around and meet your starting place it won't be as noticeable.

It should be obvious why you would start on the points marked with the x's, rather than on any other spot. They will be much less conspicuous, yielding a finer finished product.

Cutting small items.

In this book you will find some rather small lockets with very tiny pieces inside. It will be necessary to cover the blade slot in your table to keep the tiny pieces from falling through as you cut them loose.

There is very temporary method you can use if you do not plan on cutting small pieces often, and that is to take a piece of card stock and cut it about 6″ square. Cut into the blade until you have centered the piece around the blade and tape it to the table with double sticky tape.

Making a table overlay is a more permanent solution. Find a piece of 1/8″ or 1/4″ plywood slightly larger than your table. I prefer birch as this gives me a very smooth table.

Remove the blade and lay the plywood on your table. From underneath take a pencil and trace around the front, and both sided of the table shape. Remove and turn the wood piece over so you are looking at the line you just drew. Draw a line around this line about an inch away from it on the outside. (this will make the overlay slightly larger than your existing table).

Next cut the piece out on the outside line. **(see photo #10)** Cut some little 1/4″ strips and glue them flush against the outside of the inside line (you will be between the line and the edge of the overlay). This will make the table stay when you set it on the table. It won't shift.

Depending on your machine you may have to make some further cuts. If your machine has a blade clamp holder (such as the Hegners do) you will want to mark that and cut that section out, so you can still change blades without removing the insert **(see photo #11)**.

If you are lucky enough to have a slot in your table, you will want to cut that too. Use a #7 blade for this so slipping the overlay on is easy **(see photo #12)**. If you do not have a slot, put the over lay on the table and from underneath mark the spot where the blade comes through, and drill a 1/16″ hole. You will have to remove the top of your blade in order to install the overlay **(see photo #13)**.

Note: When using reverse tooth blades I do not recommend the overlay, as the added thickness will not allow the reverse teeth to come up and cut into the bottom of the wood piece.

Clamping hints:
There are so many clamping devices out on the market, one wonders which is the best.

I prefer to use Bessy clamps for small to medium projects. They are easy to use, readily available, come in many sizes, and are reasonably priced. Ask at your local tool store about them or a similar generic brand.

For the tiny little lockets that need to be glued and clamped I find common ordinary spring clothespins do a terrific job. They too are readily available and inexpensive as clamps go.

If you have no clamps, and don't wish to invest in them, you can try the old method of stacking something heavy on them. This works in a pinch for small stuff, but really doesn't do a very good job on anything larger than about 4x4″. In the long run it pays to invest in some good clamps.

Hints for storing your patterns.
Over a period of time, we seem to collect a lot of books with patterns in them. Some of the projects we actually make!. When I finally do get around to making a project, I remove the pattern section from the book make copies of the project I wish to build, and insert it as well as the original in a clear plastic binder page. Tape the page to the back of the book, inside the back cover. It will never get lost, and is right there when I am ready to use it again.

Photo 11 *Trace around shape of table from underneath.*

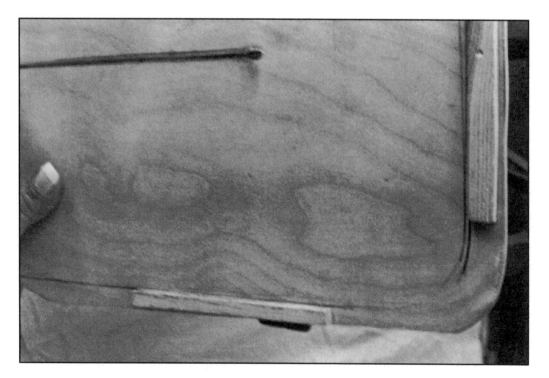

Photo 12 *Overlay table from underneath showing strips in place. This is now ready to be placed over the original table.*

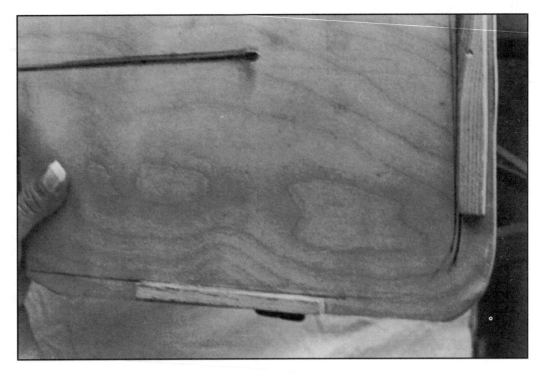

Photo 13 *Overlay in position. Cuts for blade clamp holder and table slot need to be made yet.*

For books that don't have that section to remove, just make copies of the pattern you want to make and insert it in the plastic page.

There are plastic strips you purchase that allow you to put a magazine in a regular 3 ring binder, and that is a wonderful way to store them. Mark on the binder what is inside. I have mine categorized by name of magazine, and project I want to do (i.e. Decorative Woodcrafts -Noah's ark necklace, Weekend Woodworking magazine, - Inlays . etc.)

If you have a lot of wall space in your shop, another great way to display your magazines is to nail a 2″ x 4 foot piece of pine to the wall. Screw cup hooks about every six inches into the strip.

Put a piece of cord down the center of the magazine, bring it around the back and tie a knot. Now slip the cord over one of the cup hooks, and your magazine is on view all the time.

I use one method in the house and the other method in the shop. They both work well.

Note: you can copy a pattern for your own use only. You can trace it for your own use but to copy a pattern to distribute either for free or for a fee, is against the laws of copyright.

I have tried to cover all of the questions I am constantly asked, and hope I have answered yours. If not, my address is in the back of the book on the source page. Feel free to write if you have any questions.

Chapter 3

Blades and Their Uses

BLADES

The examples shown below are in actual size, and should give the reader an idea of the tremendous variety of styles and sizes of blades that are available. The only way to learn which blade is exactly right for your job is by trial-and-error.

Remember, larger blades cut faster and last longer, while finer blades cut slower, give a smoother cut, and break more easily.

Double tooth blades are best for wood; don't try to cut metal with them.

Spiral blades do not replace standard blades, but can give you some added versatility for special projects. They cut out a lot of wood, i.e. they have a tremendous "kerf."

The Ultra blades from AMI cut faster, reduce tear-out, and decrease burning. They are expensive, but worth it!

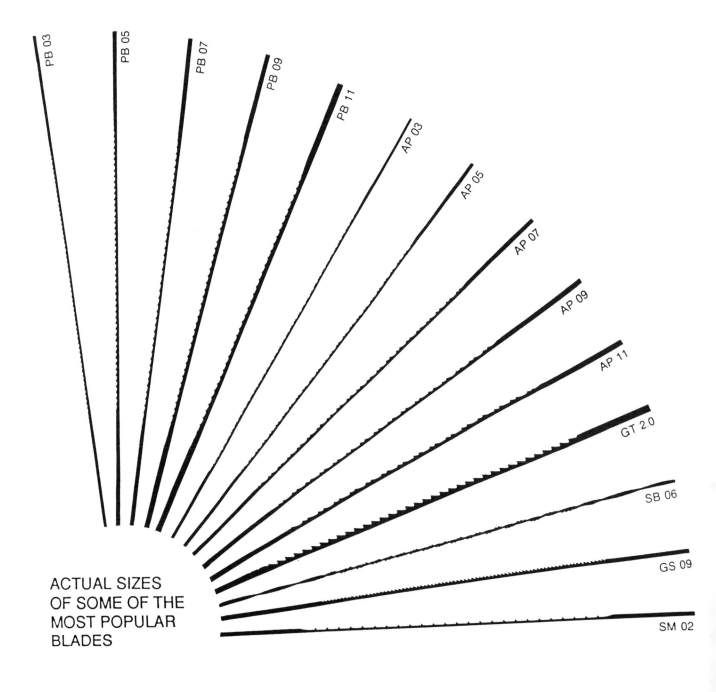

ACTUAL SIZES
OF SOME OF THE
MOST POPULAR
BLADES

BLADES AND THEIR USES

Using the right blade for the right job will make your projects go smoother, with less resistance, and give you a beautiful edge on all your projects. The wrong blade can cause undue frustration, give you a very poor cut and break often. I have included the blade chart used by Advanced Machinery Imports (AMI). This is where I buy my blades. These are also the blades referred to throughout book, so you can look at the chart to compare whatever brand you are currently using for size. The blades are illustrated actual size.

Rules of thumb for blades:

The smaller the number of the blade the smaller and thinner the blade.

The larger the number of the blade, the larger and thicker the blade.

The thinner the wood, the smaller the blade size.

The thicker the wood the bigger the blade size.

Scroll Saw Blade Reference Chart					
Blade#	Softwood	Hardwood	Metal	Glass	Alternative
AP03	up to 1/2"	Up to 1/4"	no	no	PB03
AP05	up to 3/4"	up to 1/2"	no	no	PB05
AP07	up to 1¼"	up to 3/4"	no	no	PB07
AP09	up to 1½"	up to 1"	no	no	PB09
AP11	1 to 2"	up to 1½"	no	no	PB11
GT2.0	2"	2"	no	no	SM05
SB06	1/2"	no	no	no	none
GSO9	no	no	yes	no	none
SM02	1"	1/2"	no	no	AP05

If you compare my recommendations against the actual blade chart , you will see many differences.

Scroll Saw Blade Reference Chart

Let me take you blade by blade starting with the smallest one on the chart. This is what I use each blade for. I believe just the opposite of most blade manufacturers, in that I use the smallest blade possible for the job, rather than the largest. You will find the blade system that best works for you. Between my chart and the blade chart you should be able to find the right size for your saw.

There are many sizes in between, but this will give you a general idea of what type and size of blades are available. Diamond blades are also available for your glass-cutting projects.

Blades starting with AP are double tooth blades. (I prefer these). Look at the chart and you will see two teeth, separated by a space , followed by two more teeth and so on. Blades starting with PB are "single" tooth blades. All the teeth are evenly spaced.

The SM02 is commonly known as the Ultra blade, and is a fine blade for hardwoods. It comes in three larger sizes to accommodate the thicker hardwoods. I have had mixed reports on these blades. People either love them or hate them. There does not seem to be a middle of the road.

Last but not least we have the "reverse tooth" blades. These have 4 to 6 reverse teeth on the bottom of the blade when it is mounted in the machine. These teeth come up through the bottom of the wood piece, and eliminate any and all bottom chip out. **Note**: These blades will not work on all machines, as the reverse teeth will not come up through the table. Trimming a tiny bit off the end of the blade sometimes helps, but not always. So don't go out and buy a lot of these until you have tested these at home.

Pin type blades are not listed as they are not used in any of the projects, or in my machines. A pin type blade is one that has pins going through the blade at the top and the bottom. (see diagram.) These pins are what holds the blade in the blade holder. They do not get clamped in like the straight blades do. The pin end blade limits the cutter a great amount, as it does not cut through thick wood (over 1″), and does a poor job on the 1″. It is very difficult to make a turn with this blade. Fret work that is quite delicate is an impossibility, as the pin keeps the blade from going through the very small hole we need for delicate fret work. You also cannot get a good perpendicular cut with this blade. All around it is very undesirable, and has turned many a potential scroll sawyer in to a raving maniac, trying to maneuver turns. Shy away from it! Many machines that come with this blade, have an adapter that allows you to change to the straight 5″ blades. (That has to tell you something).

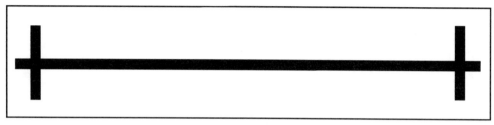

Pin type blade design

Chapter 4

MATERIALS-Choosing the Right Wood

MATERIALS-Choosing the Right Wood

There are a great many different types of wood available to woodworkers today. I have found that for scroll saw users, some woods are definitely better than others . The following chart is a basis for you to go by, drawn from my observations and experience.You will certainly want to branch out to other mediums as you advance in your techniques. As you advance in skill, you can start experimenting with other less common woods.

Wood Selection Chart

Wood	How it cuts	How it Paints	Durability
Doug Fir	Hard (grainy)	Adequate	Good
Pine	Easy	Beautifully	Adequate
Birch	Difficult	Beautifully	Excellent
Alder	Medium	Beautifully	Excellent
Oak	Hard	Only for staining.	Excellent
Redwood	Easy	Awful	Good outdoors
Cedar	Easy	Adequate	Excellent
Walnut	Medium	Stain only	Excellent
Mahogany	Stringy	Stain only	Good.
Balsa wood	Easy/soft	Adequate	Adequate
Maple	Hard	Excellent	Excellent
Cherry	Hard	Stains well	Excellent
Coco Bola	Medium	Poorly	Good
Snake Wood	Very Hard!	Poorly	Incredible!

Please bear in mind the above chart pertains to scroll saw use, and not to any other machine or medium. For example., balsa is great for carving and painting but not good for "Tole painting", and or scroll sawing, as it is too soft and too absorbent. Redwood is wonderful for outdoor furniture, making signs etc, but is not a preferred painting medium. For almost all the projects in this book, birch, and alder would do. While they are a little more difficult to cut than pine, they give you a beautiful finished edge, and paint up very nicely

Trivets, coasters and other fretwork projects made from oak are gorgeous.All they need is a coat of stain to finish beautifully. Walnut is one of the prettiest woods to make names and other lettering projects from. Your project will come off the scroll saw almost polished!

Other Materials:

Corian tile - this is a countertop material made by DuPont. It cuts beautifully and is great for small projects, outdoor items where its durability is a plus, and lettering. It is very expensive to buy, but if you are resourceful you may be able to get scrap pieces for free from a cabinet shop. The Fish Bait Cutting Board and Fish Bowl Standup Puzzle projects in this book are good examples of how this can be used.

Fabric - a great boon for quilters. By stacking fabric squares it is possible to cut out 60 to 100 pieces at a time. It is often helpful to sandwich the fabric in between two thin pieces of wood.

Paper - by sandwiching many sheets of paper together and stack cutting, you can turn out 100's of intricate snowflakes or even many types of fancy papercutting and scherenschnitte projects.

Plastic and metal - here a combination of the the right features on the saw you select and the right blades is important. Read these chapters elsewhere in the book before you begin.

Laying out your patterns with the grain

Sometimes it is critical how your pattern is put on the wood piece - whether against the grain or with the grain. Let's examine a common type of project as an example. If you are going to cut out a giraffe, you would want to put the neck of the giraffe as well as the legs running in the direction of the wood grain If you lay this project out any differently, the leg and neck pieces will break off very easily. If you look at the diagram below, you will better understand this.

Figure A. RIGHT WAY　　　　**Figure B. WRONG WAY**

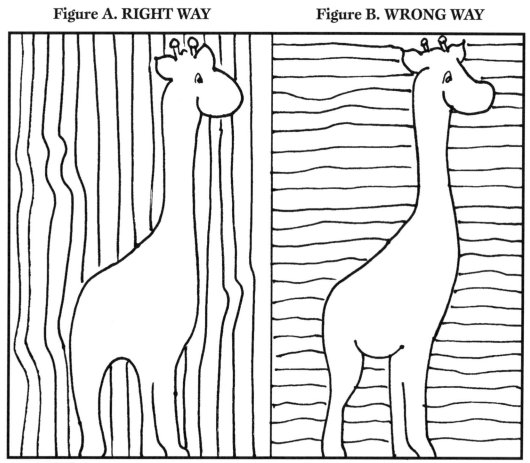

In figure A the Giraffe is placed in the proper position with the grain of the wood. The weak points are with the grain of the wood. In Figure B however you can see how easily the neck and or legs would break, as they are placed against the grain, leaving very weak points Always keep this in mind when you are setting up your patterns. Once they have been cut out it's too late to correct mistake.

Chapter 5

Scroll Saw Warm-up

If you are fairly new to scrolling or if you are not really too sure of yourself, you should do the next two "exercises" before starting any actual projects.

They are similar to those my students use in my all day seminar, and have been designed to teach many aspects of sawing.

Warm-up #1- Curves and Turns

Insert a #5 blade according to manufacturers' instructions.

Get a piece of pine approximately 8" square by 1" thick. To get the feel of the saw, freehand a few straight lines, then a few curvy ones. Once you feel comfortable, try making some very tight (360 degree) turns. Remember the pivot point I talked about earlier. (Refer to photo #7.) I told you, you would have to go back and read that section! Make sure that you are relaxed. Don't have a death grip on the wood. Practice these turns until you feel comfortable. Remember to slide your hands!

When you are ready, go on to the practice pattern.

Practice Exercise — Warm-up Pattern

Wood: 8" x 8"x 1" pine.

Blade: #5 double tooth.

Table: Square

Apply practice pattern from following page to wood with spray glue. Spray only the pattern, and spray lightly. Lines on pattern should be with the grain of the wood.

If you are right handed, start with the largest area of the wood to the right of the blade. If you are left handed start with the largest area of the wood to the left of the blade. If you do equally well with either hand, use which ever you feel comfortable with.

Start with the straight line. Notice how nearly impossible it is to follow that line? Turn your wood at a bit of a right angle to the blade, (photo #14) until you are able to follow the line more easily. (This should answer any question you may have about using a fence on a scroll saw — it cannot be done!)

Next, start cutting on the curved line. Not too fast, slow and easy does it.

It takes my beginning students nearly two full hours to complete a piece similar to this.

Remember to use the pivot point on all your turns. Complete the board. Do this over again until you feel comfortable with the saw. When you have mastered this practice pattern, pick a project and have some fun.

(I do not recommend going directly to the very tiny projects, such as the lockets just yet if you are a beginner)

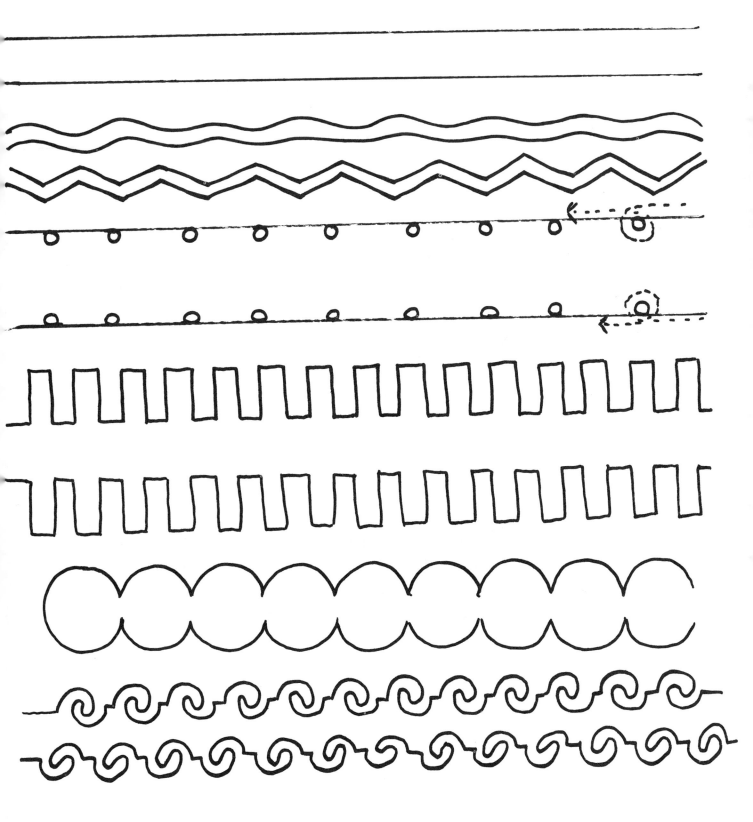

Chapter 6

PAINTING - Brushes, Materials, Basic Skills

PAINTING - Brushes, Materials, Basic Skills

First let me assure you that you do not need to be a master painter to paint the projects in this book. I have tried to keep them relatively simple so that those of you who are novice painters will be able to paint them successfully.

More advanced painters will be able to add your own embellishments to the various projects.

Basic Supplies

Let's start out with some of the basic supplies you will need to get started.

Sealer	Deltas Clear wood sealer is recommended
Graphite paper	To transfer the pattern to the wood piece.
Tracing paper	To trace the pattern from the book.
Tack Cloth	To remove dust.
Technical pen	For those who do not like working with a liner brush
Stylus	Used for making dots, transferring the pattern etc.
Palette	To put your paint out on
Palette paper	To blend the paint on
Brushes	Loew-Cornell brand brushes are what I use.
Paints	Delta Ceramcoat
Final finish	Delta clear varnish

Other supplies you will need that you can find around the house:

Water container	Paper Towels	Eraser
Pencils	Q-tips	Removable Scotch tape

I'm sure you will find other things around the house that you can use in the painting room.

I've used so many containers from my kitchen for miscellaneous stuff that I had to go out and buy new ones for the kitchen!

As you advance in your painting you will want to pick up lots more goodies but for now the above will do.

Let's take these things one by one, explain what they are used for and suggest substitutes if possible.

Sealer: All wood needs to be sealed before painting. It helps prevent warpage, weeping of knot holes, and extreme paint absorption. While sealers are many and varied, I use and recommend Deltas' Clear Wood Sealer. It dries fast and does not appear to raise the grain of the wood as much as others I have tried. It also does not have a bad odor — a decided plus for the home workshop.

Graphite paper or transfer paper: This is used to apply or transfer the pattern to the working surface. It comes in tablet form or in individual sheets. Do not mistake this for carbon paper! Graphite goes on very light and is erasable, whereas carbon goes on dark, runs when the paint hits it, and is very difficult, if not impossible, to erase.

You can make your own graphite in a pinch. (It does not work as well, and it smears a bit, but in an emergency this is how to make it.) Take a large pencil and cover a piece of paper the size you will be needing with lead. Just scribble back and forth until the paper is covered. Wipe it very gently with a Kleenex, and put it gray side down under the pattern. It works !

There are also other colors of "Transfer paper" (Graphite is always a shade of gray). You can buy them in individual sheets or tablets of mixed colors...gray, white and yellow. For those of you who sew — Please do not try to use sewing "transfer paper" it is not the same thing!

Tracing paper: This comes in several different weights. Your "normal" tracing paper is what you will find in the craft stores, and hobby shops. There is also a product called Vellum, which is used a great deal in drafting and is much heavier in weight and can cost up to twenty times as much. The only time I prefer the heavy weight is when I want to preserve a pattern indefinitely. I find the "double weight" will stand up to just about anything. It does not work as well for transferring the pattern to the wood however, as it is thicker and does not allow the pencil or stylus to penetrate without excessive pressure. If you press too hard while tracing, you can leave a permanent indentation in you wood. If you like to organize your patterns, I copy them in the copy machine using the Vellum paper. It goes through the machine without wrinkling, and becomes a permanent copy, which I then store in a clear binder page.

Tack Cloth: After wood has been sealed and sanded, it will need to be "tacked." A tack cloth is a sticky piece of gauze that you can buy in most craft and tool stores. It can be used over and over again. This is the best method for removing dust from wood.

Technical Pens: These are very useful, especially for a beginner who has not mastered the liner brush. When you must paint a very fine line, you can use 4x0 Technical pens, with much greater ease than a 10/0 liner . Many patterns call for using a pen and ink method of painting as well. Koh-I-Noor makes a wonderful set of these pens. You can also buy the disposable type at your favorite craft or hobby shop.

Stylus: The stylus is a small wooden pencil shaped tool with a metal tip on each end. One tip is small and the other is large. It is used to apply dots as well as what is commonly referred to as 'Dolly Parton or Country hearts' . Use the stylus in place of a pencil when going over the traced lines to transfer your pattern. The advantage of using a stylus for this is that it does not add an additional pencil line to your tracing, which means no distortion the next time you want to use it. The disadvantage is that you cannot readily tell where you have traced. A quick substitute for the stylus when using it for dotting is a round tooth pick, or the old stand by, sharpening the end of your liner brush in the pencil sharpener. While these make an excellent emergency stylus, the sharp tip flattens very quickly. A stylus is well worth the small investment.

Palette paper: Palette paper is used for blending the paint into the brush before applying it to the painted surface. It is critical in preparation for "floating," which is a shading method used in decorative painting. I often put the colors of paint I am using on the top section of my pallet paper as long as I am not putting out a great deal of paint. Palette paper comes in tablets. There are many brands to choose from. Be sure you get the proper palette paper for the medium you use- i.e. acrylics or oil. The projects in this book call for all acrylic paints. A suitable and very inexpensive type palette paper is common butcher paper. I cover my tables with it. Cut it into tablet size sheets, staple it and you have a palette for about one-tenth the price of store - bought ones.

Palettes: These are little round plastic dishes with "wells" to put the paint in. They are normally used for putting your "palette" (the colors you will be using) on. These again come in many forms, and I am not sure the very expensive ones are any better than the lower priced models for the everyday decorative painter. Sta-wet palettes will keep the paints moist longer with a lid that seals the whole tray to keep the paints moist indefinitely. A cheap and adequate alternative is the old fashioned meat tray. I buy meat trays in packs of 100 for around $3.25. They work well, and if you want the paints to keep moist, mist with water and cover with stretch wrap.

Brushes: There are so many brands on the market, it is really hard for a beginner to know which one to choose. Personally, I prefer Loew - Cornell brushes and use their La Corneille Golden Taklon line. They hold their sharp edges better than the other brands I have used and don't loose the spring that is so important to good brush strokes. Loew Cornell was kind enough to allow me to reprint their wonderful brush chart. You will find it on the following pages. You will also find a brush stroke study by Jackie Shaw. Jackie is a notable author of how-to books in the art of decorative painting. I purchased one of her books, and after one painting lesson was able to learn the strokes and methods I needed. I still use and carry her "Brush Stroke Work Book" in my shop, and recommend it to all of my painting students. You will find her, as well as Loew - Cornell, listed on the source page.

Do not try to use the cheap inferior brushes such as those commonly found at your local 5&10 cents store — selling 10 for a $1.00. They may be great for the children's water coloring paintings but will not do for your needs. Do not waste your time on inferior brushes. They will only frustrate you and take you much longer to master the strokes. Even with the best brushes, do not expect to master decorative painting overnight. It takes time, but with patience you will learn.

Brushes come in many sizes, and are too varied to list. As a rule, the smaller the number on the brush, the smaller the bristle. There are several brushes you will need right away for the painting projects in this book. See the basic kit listed below.

Make a list of the brushes you have by size and brand and carry it with you . (i.e., Loew Cornell #5 round etc.) This will enable you to keep track of the ones you have — you will be ready when they go on sale. Do the same thing for the paints. Delta has a wonderful little pocket-size check list you can carry with you so you will not be duplicating the paints as well. These are not only to avoid duplication - if you are in the store, buying a new book with something in it you want to paint right now, (that's always the way I feel!), you can look at the list and see if you have the proper brush sizes as well as the right paint colors.

Basic Brush Starter Kit

3/4" flat

#10 flat

#5 round

10/0 Liner

some 1" and 2" sponge brushes

1/4" deer foot brush (for stippling)

Removable Scotch tape

Q-tips

paper towels

pencils

gum or kneadable eraser

water jar

Q-tips. (or did I mention those already?) You will need a lot of these! You will find many of the things you need right in your own home. Start out with the basics, and go from there to the fancy containers, palettes, etc.

Intermediate Level Brush Kit

1" flat for base coating larger objects

#12 flat

#3 Round

#1 liner

Medium size Mop brush (not the kitchen variety) These are very much like the make-up brushes used to blend make-up. The mop is used for basically the same thing in painting.

Caring for your brushes: Brushes do not come free, so you should always spend the little extra time necessary to take proper care of them. One of the most important rules is never, never allow paint to get into the metal ferrule of the brush. If you accidentally get it in there, take the time to thoroughly wash the brush in soap and water. With your thumb nail, gently push any paint away from the metal part, and rinse the brush very well. Once it dries it is nearly impossible to get out, and the brush will be added to your "scruffy brush" collection. Scruffies are only good for stippling and such.

It is generally said that you do not need to be as concerned about the round brushes as the flat, but I still like to rinse my brush often, and try not to let paint set in the metal ferrule.

There are many commercial cleaners out there. I use Murphy's' Oil liquid soap. I have used it for many years, and my brushes thrive on it. Murphy's is available in most grocery stores.

Clean your brushes often while painting. Do not allow them to sit in water with the bristles resting against the bottom of the containers Do not use hot water to clean them. When you have finished painting clean your brushes thoroughly with soap and water, rinse well, and store with the bristles upright. Take a piece of florist foam (the green stuff florists put the flowers in to make them stand up) place in the bottom of a mason jar, and push the handle of the brush down into the foam. This is a great way to store your brushes ready for their next use.

Paints: I use Delta /Shiva Ceramcoat acrylics for all my painting. It covers well, is readily available, priced competitively, and is used by many decorative painting authors and teachers. Look in the color section of this book for the complete color painting chart for Delta Ceramcoat paints.

I have tried to keep the painting instructions simple. I hope you can all learn from them and go on to develop yourselves into fine painters. Please refer to Jackie Shaw's instructions, as they will be invaluable to you throughout this book.

*Consider joining the National Society of Decorative Painters (NSTDP).
This is a national organization devoted to bringing painters from all over the nation together to learn and share. There are many chapters throughout the United States. Check in your area to see if anything is available.
If you can not locate a chapter write the Society.*

Send inquiries to: NSTDP P.O. Box 808 Newton Kansas 67114.

Painting Tools and Materials

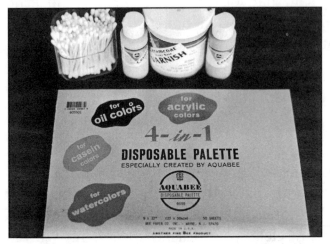

Examples from your painting kit— disposable palette, Q-tips, Delta Ceramcoat Acrylic Paints, Delta Varnish

Tracing paper, foam brushes, selection of Loew-Cornell brushes which I recommend highly. See chart on following pages for description and uses.

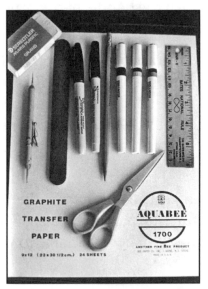

Decoration Tools (on top of Graphite Transfer Paper). From top left: Eraser, stylus, emery board, Sharpie pens, common lead pencil, Koh I Noor technical pens, six inch ruler, scissors

TWO CATEGORIES OF BRUSH STROKES:

There are two categories of brush strokes:

1. Those made with a flat brush, and —

2. Those made with a liner or a round brush.

For recording your progress in the book, practice first with the flat brush, then the liner. After you have mastered the liner, you should be able easily to do all those same strokes with the round brush. The round brush strokes will generally be a little shorter and fuller; the liner strokes, more flowing and graceful.

FLAG YOUR BRUSHES

In many cases the movement of the brush in forming a stroke is described in terms of hands on a clock. (See "S" stroke, Page 11.) To take advantage of these descriptions, you should attach a masking tape or paper flag to the tip of the brush handle as shown in Figure 1. The flag and hairs of the **flat** brush should be parallel. The flag may point any way on the **round** and **liner**. Carefully read the directions for forming each brush stroke, noting any reference to the position of the flag. If no mention is made regarding a change in position of the flag from start to finish, then the brush must not

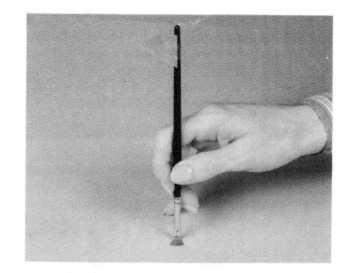

Figure 1. Attach a flag to handle of brush. With flat brush the flag is parallel to the hairs.

rotate in your fingers at all. Note the position of the flag at the beginning of the stroke. Then be sure it stays in that position throughout the stroke.

Many strokes are formed through pressure and release of pressure rather than through rotation of the brush.

Those which do involve brush rotation in your fingers are carefully described.

LOADING THE BRUSH

There are several ways of loading paint into the brush. Three of the most common, used for strokework, are described below. Of these, the easiest is the full load; and this is the one with which you should begin your studies. Later, when you can execute the strokes easily you might wish to begin experimenting with the side load and double load (primarily for flat brushes only). While the emphasis of this book is on brush **strokes** rather than brush **loading**, a brief description of the loading techniques is included below to help you further develop your skill once you've mastered the strokes.

FULL LOADING

With a little moisture in the brush, dip half the length of the hairs into the edge of a puddle of paint. Stroke the brush on the palette to work paint well up towards the metal ferrule. Stroke over and over in the same spot continually adding more paint. This action will help move the paint up **into** the brush, rather than leaving globs of paint clinging to the outside edges of the brush. Working over and over **in the same spot**

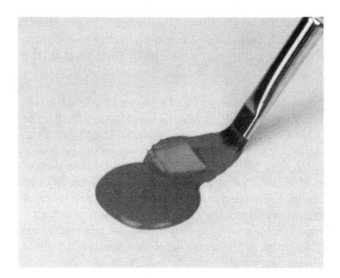

Figure 2. Full loading.

rather than stroking in different spots all over the palette, will feed the brush instead of exhausting its supply of paint. If the paint feels too stiff to move easily, add a little more moisture (water or thinner) to it. (See Figure 2.)

Figure 3. Side loading, picking up initial load of paint.

Figure 4. Side loading, "walking" the brush sideways to spread paint.

SIDE LOADING

Paint, either thick from the jar, or thinned with water to create a transparent wash, is picked up on the edge of a slightly damp brush by sliding the brush hairs alongside the puddle of paint (Figure 3). Paint is then worked gradually across the hairs to create a gradated tone ranging from intense color to a scant hint of color. This is done by stroking the brush, over and over in the same spot (no longer than 1 inch), and "walking" slightly to the right then to the left, back and forth until gradual blending is accomplished. (See Figure 4.)

Note: Until you become quite masterful in "walking" back and forth and gobbling the paint up into the hairs by applying proper pressure, "walk" only one-half the width of the brush. This will eliminate the possibility of your getting paint on the non-paint edge of the brush when you begin to "walk" back to your starting position.

It will be necessary to load more paint into the brush as it is worked both up into the hairs toward the ferrule and across the hairs toward the damp edge. Once thoroughly loaded, the brush may be quickly and easily replenished while painting with more paint or a scant bit of water. The initial loading of a color needs to be carefully done, and may take you a while to master. A drop of water on the palette is handy for restoring proper dampness to the brush. Dip the non-paint side of the brush in the water drop, then touch it briefly to a damp paper towel to remove excess water. Otherwise puddles will occur in your stroking.

DOUBLE LOADING

Follow the procedure for side loading, but this time pick up a different color on each half of the brush. Stroke the double-loaded brush on the palette as for side loading, walking left and right, until the two colors merge in the center creating a third color. For instance, if you load blue on one side, yellow on the other, after stroking and blending on the palette, you should have green in the center. (The blue and yellow should still be obvious on their respective sides.) Reload to fill the brush thoroughly, being sure, however, that no blobs cling to the brush. Paint should be worked well **into** the hairs for double loading and side loading. (See Figure 5.)

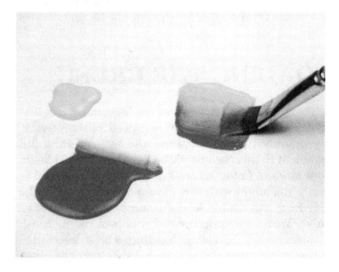

Figure 5. Double loading.

Remember, load the brush thoroughly. A couple of quick dabs in the paint puddle is not thorough. Apply pressure in loading paint into the brush by stroking firmly through the edge of the paint, permitting the brush to grab the paint and hold as much in its hairs as possible without globs clinging to the edges. So many difficulties in mastering brush control can be eliminated with proper loading techniques.

BROAD AND CHISEL STROKES

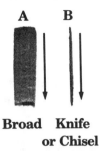

A   B

**Broad   Knife
      or Chisel**

A. This is the broad side of the brush. Used in this position, it will paint a stroke the width of the brush, or even wider if pressure is applied. Begin and end with the brush held perpendicular to painting surface. This will give clean, crisp edges.

B. The chisel stroke is done on the "knife edge" of the brush and results in a narrow, straight line. Apply **no** pressure; rather, hold the brush perpendicular and pull towards you with even pressure.

Work with these two strokes until you have good control over each. In combinations, they will be the basis of all the other flat brush strokes you learn in this book. Once you've mastered them, pulling the strokes toward you, try pulling to the left and the right and away from you. Some directions will be easier for you than others.

Now you try it. Thin paint very slightly with water. Record your progress. Jot down today's date.

Make a real effort to keep your brush handle perpendicular to the painting surface. Strive for crisp, even lines and edges. Extra effort in developing control now will pay off later.

WHOOPS! Study your first painted samples above. Look for any trouble spots as illustrated below. Mark the troublesome areas with a pen as a reminder where to direct your attention.

Hey, where's your self control? You had a nice beginning but in your eagerness to get through, you forgot to slow down, stop, let hairs return to a chisel edge, then lift off.	Two factors could cause ragged edges. 1) Brush is not held perpendicular — laying too flat to painting surface. 2) Brush is in bad condition causing hairs to separate.

Bulges are caused by uneven pressure.	Pressure is too heavy. Skim along painting surface.	Brush is not in good condition. Dried paint has been allowed to remain near ferrule causing the brush hairs to bulge.	Haphazard practicing. Slow down. Be precise.

Now then, with all your trouble spots noted, turn to the Magic Paper on page 9 and practice with water. Later today, tomorrow, or next week when you feel you have greatly improved, return to this page and paint a follow-up sample. Be sure to date it and record your progress.

SCROLL AND FLAT COMMAS

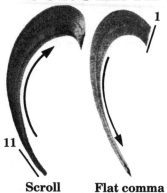

Scroll **Flat comma**

These two strokes look very similar but are made quite differently. Both use the chisel and broad strokes.

The **scroll** stroke (usually the more difficult of the two for beginners) begins with a chisel stroke and curves, flattening out into a broadstroke. It begins with the flag pointing to 11 o'clock. Try not to move the flag at all when making the stroke. To paint a stroke in the other direction, hold the flag at 1 o'clock.

The **flat comma,** on the other hand, begins with a broad stroke, curves slightly, and with gradual release of pressure, slides into a chisel stroke. Begin with the flag at 1 o'clock. A **very slight** rotation - no more than from 1 back to 11 o'clock - may be helpful.

You will likely find you prefer one of these strokes over the other. Never mind. Learn them both! Then also practice them in other directions - facing the opposite way as well as upside down. When you get expressive and fancy later, you will find that the scroll stroke lends itself to freer designing; the flat comma, to a bit more controlled effort. Practice here first, to give yourself a basis from which to review your growth. Write in the date.

WHOOPS! Did you encounter any of these common problems? Mark the mistakes on your work above. Learn to critique your work positively. You'll improve **because** of your mistakes.

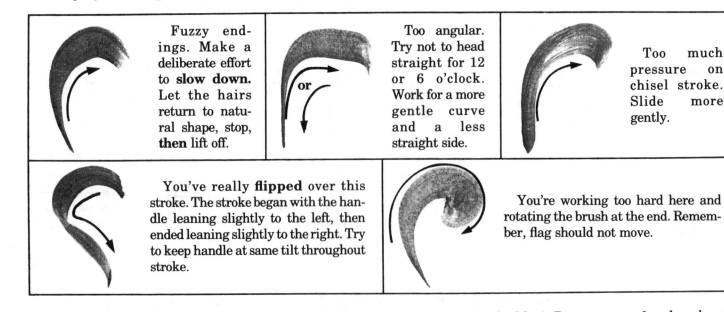

Fuzzy endings. Make a deliberate effort to **slow down.** Let the hairs return to natural shape, stop, **then** lift off.

Too angular. Try not to head straight for 12 or 6 o'clock. Work for a more gentle curve and a less straight side.

Too much pressure on chisel stroke. Slide more gently.

You've really **flipped** over this stroke. The stroke began with the handle leaning slightly to the left, then ended leaning slightly to the right. Try to keep handle at same tilt throughout stroke.

You're working too hard here and rotating the brush at the end. Remember, flag should not move.

Now with all that knowledge — of the things that can go awry — head for the Magic Paper on page 9 and work out the kinks. When you can see and feel progress, return to this page to record your successes.

WARM UP LINER EXERCISE: SPIRAL LINER AND ROUND BRUSH

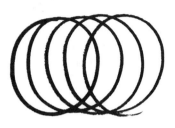

If you're old enough to remember the Palmer Method of handwriting, this exercise may look familiar. It is a good one to help you develop flowing motion, and steady, even control of the liner brush. **Think round and paint round.** Develop a rhythm as you paint the spirals, trying to space each loop evenly. Hold the brush perpendicular to the painting surface. Work from the tip of the brush and be sure that the loops are formed by the motion of your whole arm from your shoulder, not by your fingers. Imagine that your thumb and forefingers are immobile. Balance on your little finger, being sure that it **moves** with the rest of your arm. And remember, the brush hairs should always **follow** the handle.

Thin your paint to an almost ink-like consistency. Thoroughly load the brush and try to paint as long a spiral as possible with one loading.

Strive for uniformity of thickness, rhythm, and size (about the size of a quarter).

WHOOPS! Well, how did you do? Study your first effort above. Compare it to the problem samples below. Review the directions at the top of the page and learn to critique your own work.

Inflation is so bad you've forgotten how big a quarter is. Don't be so uptight. Stretch the loops a little larger.

Little angular glitches like these may appear anywhere in the loop, and are caused by either: 1) moving thumb and fingers to **push** brush around rather than working from shoulder; 2) hesitating at the top and thinking "whew, I got to the top, now I go back down," thus; 3) forgetting to think **around** or over the top, and then down.

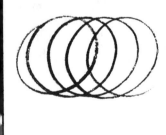

Paint is too dry or brush is insufficiently loaded. Paint should be quite thin, so it can feed through the brush hairs like ink in a pen reservoir. The brush should be thoroughly loaded until it can hold no more paint. Painting too fast can also cause skipped places.

Where's the fire? Slow down. Be precise, rhythmic, uniform. You can become expressive and unique after you've mastered the techniques.

If you've isolated your weak areas, then turn to the MAGIC PAPER on page 9, and work out the kinks. Come back when you've improved and record your progress here.

CRESCENT STROKE

This stroke, by itself, can be used to make flowers, or it may embellish the crescents made with the flat brush. Like the "S," the stroke begins on the tip of the brush. Be sure the brush is held perpendicular to the painting surface. Think of a circle as you make the stroke. Pull slightly; then gradually apply pressure, curving around; and gradually release pressure. The stroke progresses from thin to thick to thin again. Emphasise the thick and thin. Contrast makes these strokes interesting.

Thin paint slightly, and load brush thoroughly. Do you remember always to balance on your little finger? And does the little finger move with the rest of your arm and shoulder? If it gets stuck, then you'll have to **push** the brush with your thumb and fingers and that's a No No!

WHOOPS! Before checking the problem areas below, study your strokes and see if you can analyze any problems on your own. Begin now to develop a critical eye.

Too heavy handed in the beginning. Start on the tip of the brush. Apply pressure in the center top as you go up and over.	Croquet anyone? Corners are squared. Think **round,** up and **over.** No corners!
Ends are too closed. Open it up a bit. Be more careful at the ending.	You started off so well here that you got excited and hurried through the ending. Remember to slow down, let hairs come back to a point, stop, then lift off.

There now. With an understanding of where the weak spots are, go directly to the Magic Paper. With your cooperation, it will help you iron out the problems.

COMMA STROKE

head

tail

This is a stroke you'll have a lot of fun with. It makes nice borders, marvelous flowers, even moustaches and hairdos. Make it with thick paint for a richly textured stroke. Or, thin the paint slightly for a somewhat flatter stroke. Load extra paint on the tip of the brush to create a nice, rounded "head" on the stroke. Press the loaded brush down on the painting surface, causing hairs to flare out a little; pause; then begin pulling and releasing pressure on the brush. Slow down as you near the tip of the "tail" of the stroke, letting hairs return to the point. Stop, then lift off. Try the strokes curving to left, to right, straight up, sideways, and upside down.

Practice comma strokes large and small, in all directions. Remember to record the date.

WHOOPS!

Still in a hurry, eh? When will you learn to slow down! Let the brush hairs return to their natural configuration, stop, **then** lift off. You can also get fuzzy "tails" from bad brushes - ones which no longer come to a fine point. Have you let paint dry and harden in your brush up in the metal ferrule? See page 22.	A point on the head of the stroke can result from: 1) having failed to load extra paint on the tip, particularly on the fine pointed liners; 2) pulling the stroke as soon as the brush was set down without pausing to permit hairs to spread to form the rounded head.

Did you forget how to release pressure gradually? Too sudden a release of pressure causes abrupt changes as shown here. Let your little finger act as a lever to help raise your whole hand (and thus the brush), gradually decreasing pressure.

Mark your trouble spots in the practice strip above, then turn to page 9 to practice. Make a follow-up sample here when you're nearly great.

TEARDROP STROKE

This stroke, at first glance, looks very much like a comma stroke. But, as you will observe when you paint samples of each, the teardrop has a little collection of paint which is deposited in the head, whereas the paint flows smoothly through the head of the comma stroke. The teardrop is begun on the tip of the brush at the tip of the "tail" of the stroke. Pull and gradually press to form "head." Lift straight off. Keep brush perpendicular to your painting surface.

Hint: Load more paint in the middle of the brush. Stroke excess paint out of the tip onto the palette. This is a very spontaneous stroke once you've mastered it.

Practice these straight as illustrated, to start. Later, curve them and do them sideways and upside down. Thin paint slightly, (light cream consistency).

WHOOPS! There are several things that can go awry when you first start making this stroke. How many problems can you locate in your first practice sample.

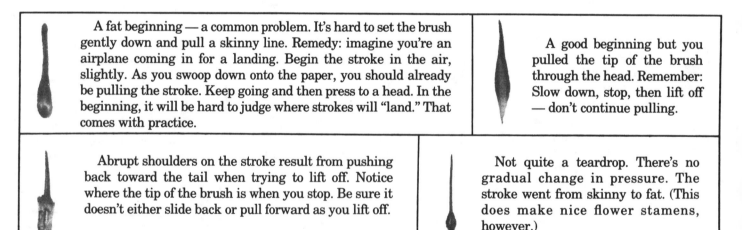

A fat beginning — a common problem. It's hard to set the brush gently down and pull a skinny line. Remedy: imagine you're an airplane coming in for a landing. Begin the stroke in the air, slightly. As you swoop down onto the paper, you should already be pulling the stroke. Keep going and then press to a head. In the beginning, it will be hard to judge where strokes will "land." That comes with practice.

A good beginning but you pulled the tip of the brush through the head. Remember: Slow down, stop, then lift off — don't continue pulling.

Abrupt shoulders on the stroke result from pushing back toward the tail when trying to lift off. Notice where the tip of the brush is when you stop. Be sure it doesn't either slide back or pull forward as you lift off.

Not quite a teardrop. There's no gradual change in pressure. The stroke went from skinny to fat. (This does make nice flower stamens, however.)

This is a great stroke to practice on Magic Paper. Remember to be an airplane and glide in for a landing. Paint a follow-up sample below once you're satisfied with your progress.

BRUSH SHAPES AND THEIR USES

The descriptions here use generally accepted terminology developed and/or used in the tole and decorative painting field. Fine artists may use different terms for brushes and techniques which are the same or quite similar. Although the uses described and shown may be applicable to watercolors and oils, we elected to base our information on acrylics because of their wide ranging popularity at all skill levels.

All brushes shown are part of our La Corneille-Golden Taklon brush line. Many of the shapes are also available in other hair types as well.

Shape	Common Uses
Round-7000	Thick to thin strokes can be made by variation of pressure; use for detail work or filling in large areas depending on the brush size used and pressure. Commonly used brush for stroke work and borders in folk art and rosemaling. Examples: comma and S-strokes. Also watercolor wash effects.
Spotter-7650	Very fine detail work. Examples: tiny stroke work, eyes, eyelashes, dots, signatures. Working in miniature.
Tight Spot Detailer-7670	Bent handle on this spotter allows the painter more maneuverability in hard to reach places and also allows additional visibility in work as the painter's hand is no longer directly over the area of painting. Use when working inside of things such as ceramic pieces or baskets.
Liner-7350	Continuous curved or straight lines of the same thickness when uniform pressure is used, or vary pressure to create thin to thick lines. Examples: monogramming, highlighting, outlining, stroke work. Paint should be thinned to an ink-like consistency.
Ultra Round-7020	Continuous scrolling and straight line work, script calligraphy. Use as a liner with thinned, ink-like paint staying up on the tip. The Ultra Round's full belly acts as a reservoir allowing continuous line work without frequent reloading. Slight pressure can be applied to vary line thickness, but belly hairs will flare out if too much pressure is applied.

Script Liner-7050	Long hairs hold more liquid than a liner, but also require more control. Use to create long scrolling, straight lines, or stroke work. Use pressure to change thicknesses.
Shader-7300	Use on flat or chisel edge. Sharp square shape creates crisp edges and offers precision control in tight areas. Use for: stroke work - comma, "S," and"C;" filled circles; double load; side load to float or walk color; wash effects; blend color; block in large areas of color without ridges of paint.
Angular Shader-7400	Use for: "S", fan, leaf, and C strokes; to create leaves, roses, and rosebuds. Like a shader, can be double, single, and side loaded. Angled shape is suited to painting or blending in small areas and corners.
Chisel Blender-7450	Thick, heavy color; short, controlled strokes, fine precision blending.
Wash-7550	Large, broad sweeping strokes, washes, base coating or applying finishes.
Filbert-7500	Rounded shape creates soft edges; blend colors as on cheeks; fill in areas; natural shape for many flower petals, leaves, and bird and duck feathers.

BRUSH SHAPES AND THEIR USES

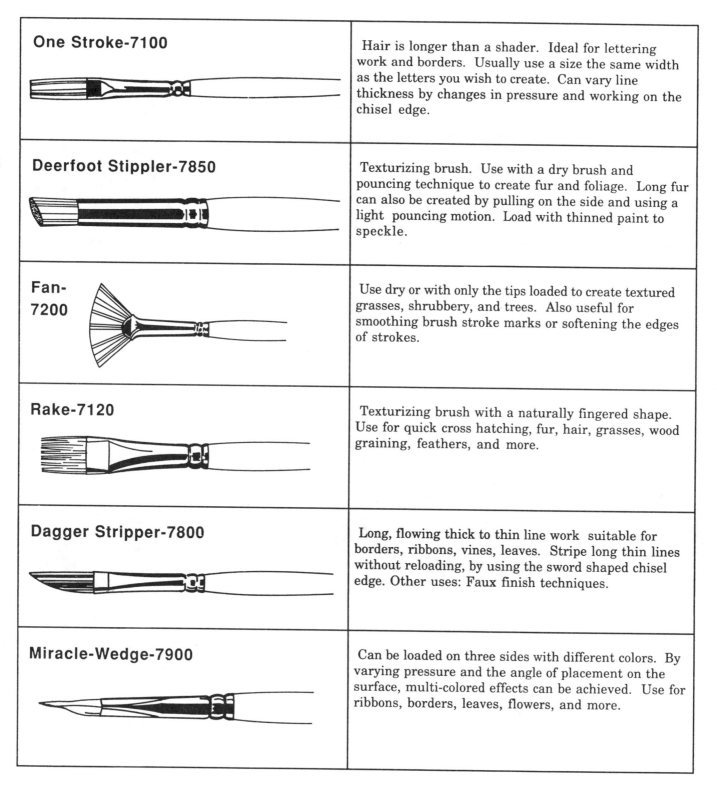

One Stroke-7100	Hair is longer than a shader. Ideal for lettering work and borders. Usually use a size the same width as the letters you wish to create. Can vary line thickness by changes in pressure and working on the chisel edge.
Deerfoot Stippler-7850	Texturizing brush. Use with a dry brush and pouncing technique to create fur and foliage. Long fur can also be created by pulling on the side and using a light pouncing motion. Load with thinned paint to speckle.
Fan-7200	Use dry or with only the tips loaded to create textured grasses, shrubbery, and trees. Also useful for smoothing brush stroke marks or softening the edges of strokes.
Rake-7120	Texturizing brush with a naturally fingered shape. Use for quick cross hatching, fur, hair, grasses, wood graining, feathers, and more.
Dagger Stripper-7800	Long, flowing thick to thin line work suitable for borders, ribbons, vines, leaves. Stripe long thin lines without reloading, by using the sword shaped chisel edge. Other uses: Faux finish techniques.
Miracle-Wedge-7900	Can be loaded on three sides with different colors. By varying pressure and the angle of placement on the surface, multi-colored effects can be achieved. Use for ribbons, borders, leaves, flowers, and more.

Chapter 7

Puzzles

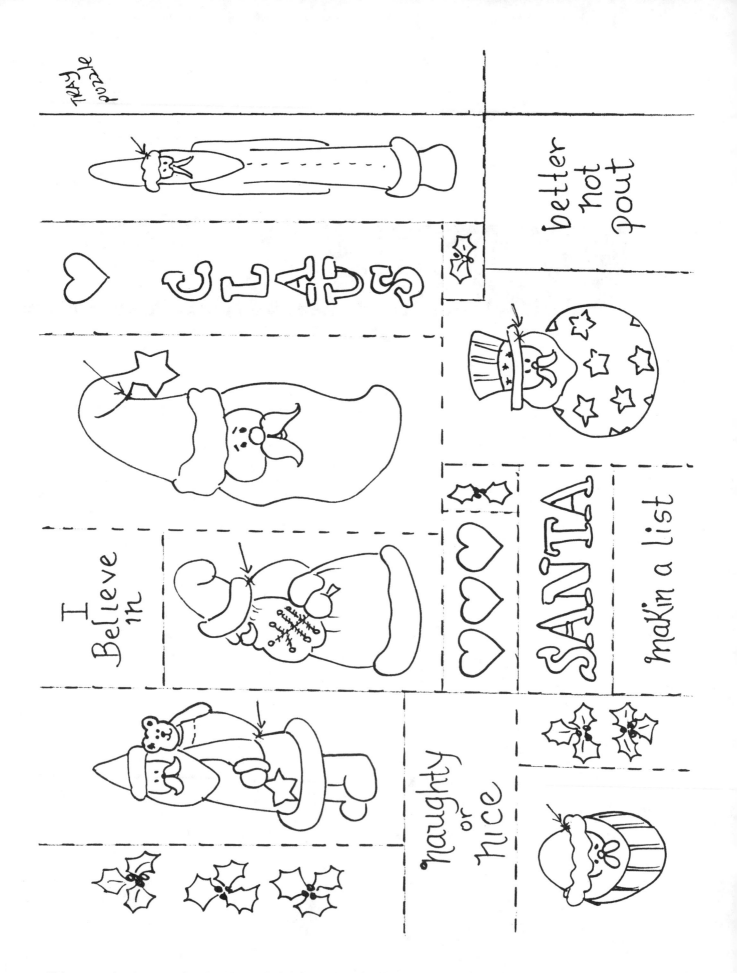

TRAY PUZZLE

better not pout

SANTA ♥

I Believe in

SANTA

makin a list

naughty or nice

PUZZLES

CHRISTMAS TRAY PUZZLE

See color section for full color photograph of completed project.

I fell in love with this pattern when I first saw it painted on a pillow. I immediately visualized it as a little tray puzzle. I approached the original designer, and this is the result! A very special thanks to Kathie Rueger of "Country Sunshine" for allowing me to adapt her adorable patterns to wood. Kathie is very talented, and has many pattern packets as well as books available for your enjoyment. For more information on how to contact Kathie see the source page.

These instructions will also serve as general instructions for all the tray puzzles in this book.

Wood: **10 " x 13" x 1/2" Pine**
            10" x 13" x 1/8" Birch ply

Center pattern on the pine, and tape the two pieces of wood together. **(Photo #20)**. Cut out around perimeter.

Untape the wood. Set the thinner piece of wood aside. Drill very tiny pilot holes where marked by an X, on the 1/2″ pine piece. These holes are just large enough for the blade to fit through.

Insert the blade through the bottom of the wood piece. **(Photo #21)** Re-install the blade into the upper blade clamp, **(photo #22)** and cut the piece out. Remove each piece and set aside as you finish it. Note proper hand positioning while cutting **(photo #23)**, and proper position for your index finger while approaching and executing turns. **(Photo #24)**. Complete all cuts in the same manner.

Leave the pieces out, **(photo #25)** and run a line of yellow wood glue on the back of the pine piece, **(photo #26)**. Align the two pieces up, and clamp together with clothespins.

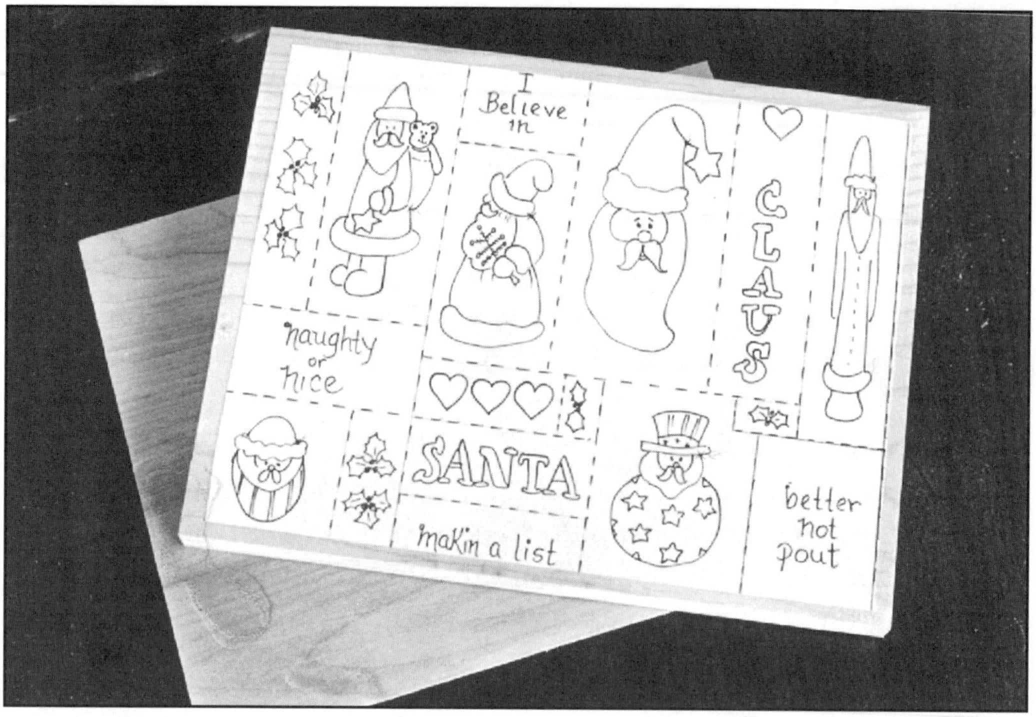

Photo # 20   *Christmas Tray Puzzle pattern centered on 1/2 " pine. Birch ply backing in background.*

Photo #21   *Inserting the blade through pilot hole from the back of the piece. Do this to cut out all interior figures.*

Photo #22 *Blade re-attached in upper clamp ready for sawing. Note optional quick clamp accessory attachment. This is very useful when making many inside cuts.*

Photo #23 *Cutting out the different Santa interior pieces. Note proper hand positioning for safety...*

Photo #24   *... and important "pivot point" placement of finger behind blade.*

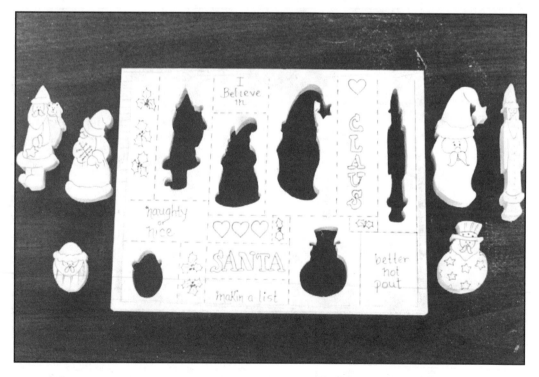

Photo #25   *All interior pieces are cut out. Piece is now ready to have backing glued on.*

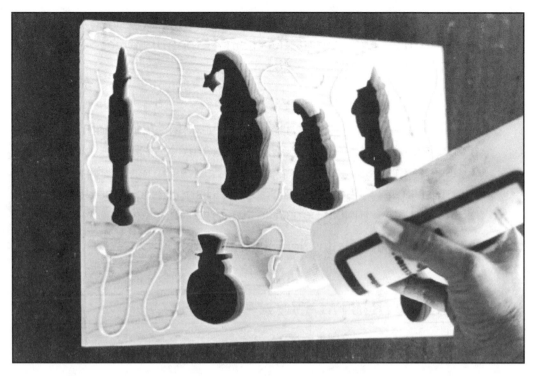

Photo #26   *Make sure you apply enough glue to all areas to make a good tight bond.*

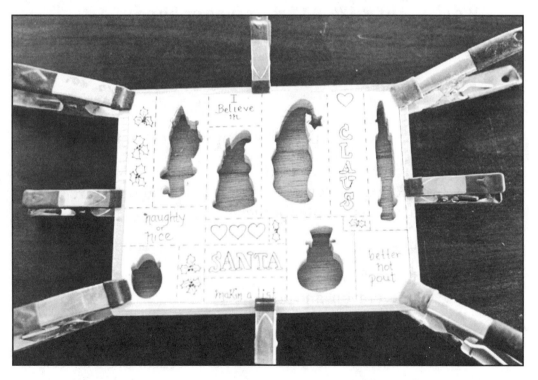

Photo #27   *These spring clamps work well to clamp pine and backing together while glue sets. You may need to pad some varieties of clamps to avoid marking the wood surface.*

(Photo #27). Wipe off any excess glue that may ooze out, and allow to dry. Sand the cut pieces on the bottom if necessary with an emery board **(photo #28).**

Insert Santas and sand.

Paint however you wish. Refer to color gallery photograph if you wish to follow my example. Be sure to seal the wood first. This is a very easy piece to paint, as Santas' are rather basic. (No offense Santa!) The thin wording and stitches can be done in black with a technical pen or a "Sharpie" marker.

Finish with Delta Clear Satin Varnish.

GIRLS CHRISTMAS TREE PUZZLE

Cutting Instructions

Blade   **#3 if using pine — tension 1/2 to 3/4 turn**
               #5 if using birch — tension normal
Wood   **10"x 12" x 1" clear pine or birch.**
               Birch is far more durable, but slightly more difficult to cut.
Table   **Square**

Make copy of the pattern and apply with spray glue to your wood piece.

Cut the outside perimeter first, then cut and remove the toy pieces that sit on the outer branches.

(Not including the clown on the top, this stays attached.)

Cut the three separate sections of the tree apart, then the house, bottle, crayon, and dog.

Lastly, cut off the tree stand.

Sand all the pieces carefully where needed. Use a tack cloth to wipe off the sawdust. Seal with Delta clear wood sealer. Allow to dry. Sand again very lightly if needed. Tack again before painting.

SCHOOL

© Joanne Lockwood 88'

TEA

BABY

CRAYONS

©Jeanne Lockwood '92'

Photo #28 *Emery boards (from beauty supply house) are ideal for this type of sanding job.*

I have deliberately left the pieces plain, so that if you do not want to paint them, they are still recognizable. If you want them painted you may use a non-toxic paint such as Delta Ceramcoat.

You could even let a child use color crayons and do their own little things on the pieces. (It's a lot less messy too!)

PLEASE NOTE!

If you are considering making this puzzle for small children that have a tendency to put things in their mouths, I would enlarge the pattern. Make it from 2″ wood instead and use a #9 blade for cutting.

BOYS CHRISTMAS TREE PUZZLE

Cutting Instructions

This is cut from the same size wood as the Girls Christmas tree puzzle.

Make copy of the pattern and apply with spray glue.

Cut the outside perimeter first, and then cut and remove all the pieces that sit on the edges or close to the edges of the tree branches.

Cut the outside star away from the top of the tree. Set each piece aside as you cut.

Now cut in between the branches removing the Teddy, the ball and the bus. Cut the tree stand off.

Sand and seal all pieces. An emery board comes in handy for this. Tack each piece. Seal the wood first if you are planning on painting the project. Lightly tack again before continuing.

The same thing applies to this puzzle as all others. If you intend using for a small child that still puts things in his or her mouth, enlarge the pattern, use two inch pine and a #9 blade.

GIANT ICE CREAM CONE PUZZLE

See color section for full color photograph of completed project.

Cutting instructions

Blade:	**#9 double tooth**
Wood:	**17" x 6" x 2" pine**
Table:	**Square**

Special instructions: Be sure to feed the wood square into the blade. **(Photo # 18)** Do not push the blade off to the left or the right as you turn the piece **(photo #19)**. This may cause the

puzzle pieces not to fit properly, or they may not even fit at all.

Make a copy of the pattern and with spray glue attach it to the wood piece. The grain needs to be running the long way. (From top to bottom of puzzle.)

Cut out the outside perimeter first — if you have a router, use a 1/2" roundover bit and round over the ice cream part of the cone. Next you will cut the scoops apart beginning with the cherry and ending up with the cone.

Cut slowly and try not to stop and start except at the edges where each scoop meets another. Every time you stop, you leave a mark that will need sanding later. If you cut too fast, you will also have to sand later. By cutting slowly and steadily, you will save you extra work in the long run. After all the pieces are cut out, sand lightly to prepare for sealing and painting.

GIANT ICE CREAM CONE *Painting directions*

Palette: Delta Ceramcoat	
Golden Brown	**White**
Autumn Brown	**Coral**
Luscious Lemon	**Apple Green**
Pretty Pink	**Tropic Bay**
Napthol Crimson	**Rouge**
Yellow	

Brushes needed: **1" Flat (or foam brush)**
#12 Flat   #2 script

Since there is very little design to this piece, you can probably free hand the crisscrosses, and the word "Cone". If you have trouble with this, trace the pattern. Apply it to the wood with graphite paper.

Cone: Base with a mix GB + W + AB (put a puddle of white on your palette, add a couple of drops of GB, and a drop of AB). Mix and paint the cone with the 1" flat or foam brush.

Scoops: Base each scoop in a different color as follows (starting at bottom next to cone then working your way to the top) Coral...LL....AG.....PP.....TB.....NC.

Shade all scoops on top and bottom with the #12 flat as follows.

C. scoop: Shade with R

LL. scoop...Shade with Y.

AG scoop...Shade with AG + W (1-2 ratio.) These will be a lighter shade than the scoop.

PP scoop...Shade with H.

TB scoop...Shade with TB + W (1-2 ratio)

Drips: These are done with the #2 script brush.

Paint the drips in the same color as the scoop itself. Dip the liner brush in the appropriate color, after having slightly watered the colors down. Leave a little blob of paint on the end of it. Set the tip of the brush down on the scoop, press slightly to allow blob of paint to adhere to surface, and very slowly pull the brush up on the tip of the bristle pulling towards you, while using a "shaky hand motion" to form the "trail" of the drip. You may want to practice this if you have never done it before. ***Hint:*** Keep the brush in a 90 degree position. Do not hold it like a pencil.

Shade on the right side of each drip with the same color you floated the scoop with.

Write cone with liner or script and AB + GB

Now go back to the cone, and sand it lightly with crumpled brown paper. (Grocery bags)

Float the pattern of the cone in AB + GB (ratio 1-1) with your #12 flat.

Above:
Two exciting new techniques for scroll saw woodcrafters.

Left: **Teddy Bears Basket** Collapsible baskets are a fun challenge. Basket is cut from a single piece of wood in one long continuous cut. See Baskets chapter for specific instructions and two ready to use patterns to try on your own.

Right: **Southwest Design 3-D Scene** - 3-Dimensional Scenes are also cut from a single piece of wood. The cut is slightly beveled, allowing pieces to "pop" in and out. Also see Heart Country Scene in photographs below.

Bottom Left
Heart Country 3-D Scene: See 3-D Chapter for complete instructions, pattern and painting instructions.

Bottom Right
Back view of Heart Country 3-D project. Notice how the different segments slide in or out and lock into place.

Top Left
Grandchildren Hanging Plaque (from Fretwork Chapter). Put the individual names of each of your grandchildren on the hanging hearts for a special family memento.

Below Right
Painted Christmas Snowflake Ornament (from Christmas Projects Chapter). *"Butterflies & Flowers"* pattern from Fretwork Chapter. Notice how a nice set of coasters with matching trivet can be made from the same basic pattern.

Bottom Left
Trivets made from *"Hearts & Flowers Pattern"* (right) and *"Hearts with Diamonds"* pattern (left). These are made from oak which finishes easily and beautifully. See Fretwork Chapter. (Bottom) **Fish Bait Cutting Board** (More Neat Projects Chapter). This is made from Corian tile. See Materials chapter for more information on using Corian for different projects.

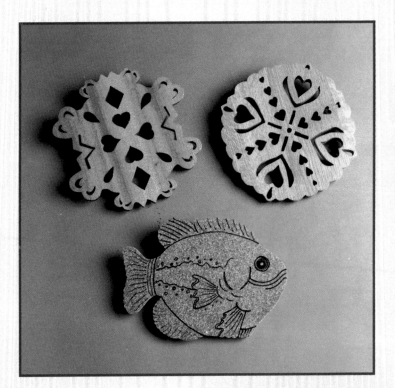

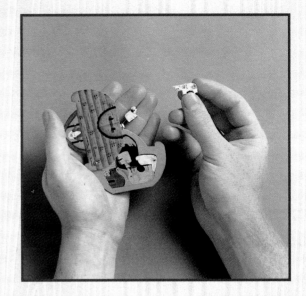

You will not be able to keep up with the demand for these!

Top Left

Small Wonders™ Projects: clockwise from top right- **Cookie Jar, Primitive Noah's Ark, Teddy Pin, Teddy Bear and Babies** (also showing separate pieces before assembly and painting) **Easter Bunny.** If you take your time and follow the patterns and instructions inside this book faithfully, you will be able to make these delightful small puzzle/lockets.

Bottom Left

Cow Tray Puzzle made from the pattern and instructions in the Puzzles chapter. Children are intrigued by the top which slides open to reveal an assortment of miniature dairy items to remove and play with.

Top Right

Here's a close up of the Primitive Noah's Ark puzzle/locket showing you its relative size and beautifully simple design.

Bottom Right

More Small Wonders™ puzzle/lockets. *Clockwise from top right —***Three Bears, Dolly's House, Fine Feathered Friends.** *Top Left—* **Favorite Teddy Ring Box** made from pattern in More Neat Projects chapter.

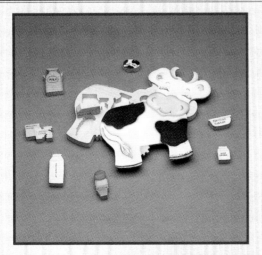

Scroll Saw Woodcrafting Magic
Color Project Gallery

by Delta

The colors represented here may be affected by age, light and printing methods and may vary slightly from actual paint colors. Variations in surface texture, lighting and application may also influence the color effect of the painted surface.

GLEAMS
CERAMCOAT ACRYLICS

2001 Antique White
2017 Queen Anne's Lace
2401 Lt. Ivory
2092 Old Parchment
2505 White
2454 Western Sunset
2036 Ivory
2101 Pineapple
2460 Putty
2064 Sunbright Yellow
2005 Pale Yellow
2027 Bright Yellow
2448 Custard
2004 Luscious Lemon
2504 Yellow
2043 Tangerine
2459 Crocus
2041 Bittersweet
2042 Pumpkin
2408 Napthol Crimson
2412 Empire Gold
2503 Bright Red
2026 Orange
2077 Cardinal Red
2076 Crimson
2056 Berry Red
2409 Napthol Red Lt.
2458 Nectar
2083 Fire Red
2098 Tomato Spice
2404 Rouge
2020 Red Iron Oxide
2107 Tompte Red
2045 Fiesta Pink
2044 Coral
2061 Pink Angel

2605 Red Copper
2617 Orange Pearl Finish
2603 Silver
2615 Sunshine Pearl Finish
2614 Aqua Cool Pearl Finish
2601 Pearl Finish
2609 Bobby Blue Pearl Finish
2600 Metallic Gold
2623 Violet Pearl Finish
2607 Copper
2622 Fuchsia Pearl Finish
2606 Bronze
2612 Pinkie Pearl Finish
2602 Kim Gold
2084 Lisa Pink
2604 14K Gold
2449 Hydrangea
2624 Pale Gold
2461 Pink Frosting
2437 Rose Mist
2018 Indiana Rose
2129 Gypsy Rose
2132 Bouquet
2046 Adobe
2464 Sachet
2130 Sweetheart Blush
2450 Rose Cloud
2075 Maroon
2088 Pretty Pink
2406 Mendocino
2405 Dusty Mauve
2443 Napa
2469 Antique Rose
2128 Dusty Purple
2434 Vintage Wine
2048 Grape
2060 Lilac
2456 Dusty Plum
2467 Wisteria
2091 GP Purple
2047 Lavender
2403 Lilac Dusk
2502 Phthalo Blue
2015 Purple
2089 Navy Blue

Colors

Left
Fish Bowl Stand Up Puzzle: See Puzzles Chapter for pattern and painting instructions. This is made from Corian tile but can also be made from wood. Also attractive when left unpainted.

Bottom
Sail Fish 3-D Scene. Another project using Corian tile. The 3-D relief effect really brings this pattern to life.

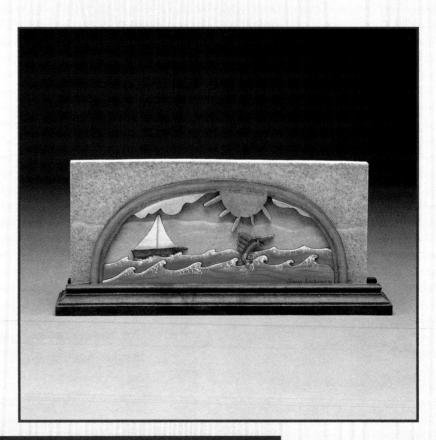

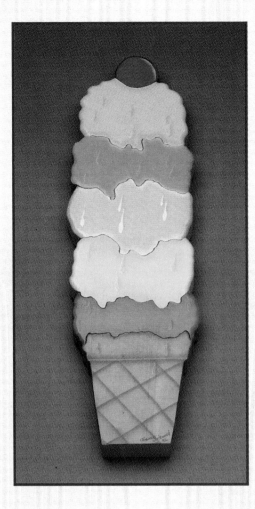

Above
Honey Pot Bank - (More Neat Projects Chapter) You can also buy a simple insert that turns this into a musical bank - playing a song whenever your child deposits money.

Left
Giant Ice Cream Cone -(Puzzles Chapter)

Bottom
Tic Tac Toe Teddy - (More Neat Projects Chapter) Dowel pins in each corner for storage keep these little teddy markers from getting lost.

Top Left
Fun Holiday Projects! (Christmas Projects Chapter) **Merry Christmas Fretwork , Santa Door Greeting,Christmas Tray Puzzle.**

Bottom Left
Tray Puzzles. You can make these as simple or complex as you wish for different age groups. See Puzzles Chapter.

Bottom Right
Apple Alphabet Necklace
(Alphabets & Things Chapter)

When everything is dry, lightly sand again with the paper bag.

Finish with Delta clear satin varnish. The sponge brush can be used for this, but don't press so hard that you leave bubbles on the cone!

Your loved ones will enjoy this for years to come.

COW TRAY PUZZLE

See the color section for a full color photograph of the completed project.

Cutting directions

Blade: **Size #5 for outside cutting. #3 for doing the inside cuts.**

Wood: **1 pc. 8" x 7" x 1/8" Baltic birch. (you may use birch door skin)**

1 pc. 8" x 7" x 1/4" Baltic Birch.

1 pc. 8" x 7" x 1/2" Pine

Table: **Square.**

Additional Supplies needed:

1/4" x 1/2" long round head wood screw

Heavy cording for tail (optional)

Yellow wood glue

Cut all pieces to the exact size. Stack together as follows:

Bottom: 1/8" with good side down.

Center: 1/2" pine.

Top: 1/4" with best side up. Bind on the edges with 3/4" masking tape. Make copy of cow patterns and apply the front of the cow on to the top wood piece with spray glue.

Insert a #5 blade into the machine, and cut out the outside perimeter of the cow. Separate the pieces, and set the two thin sections aside.

Apply the center portion of the pattern to the 1/2″ piece. Drill a very tiny hole at the corner edge of each puzzle piece — just large enough for the #3 blade to fit through.

Install the bottom only of the #3 blade, insert the top of the blade through one of the pilot holes. (Insert blade from underside of wood.) Attach the blade to the upper clamp, tension the machine, and cut the piece out. Remove and set aside. Repeat these steps for all other pieces.

When you have them all cut out, set them aside. Now put a line of yellow wood glue on the bottom side of the center piece. Put it on top of the bottom section, move it around slightly to spread the glue, line it back up, and clamp in place. (Bessy or spring clamps work well for this).

Look for any glue drips at this time, and if you find any, wipe them off with a damp cloth. Pay particular attention to the little sections the products go back into. If you allow a hump of glue to dry inside, the pieces will not fit back in properly. Use a wet Q-tip to clean out these areas.

When everything is dry, sand, tack and seal the piece and prepare for painting.

Either drill the hole for the screw now, or wait until after it is painted.

If you want to make a tail instead of painting one on, get several pieces of cord, or heavy string, braid it and glue the end that will be going into the cow. Drill a hole where the tail should be, just large enough to force the tail into. Insert the tail after all other pieces have been painted.

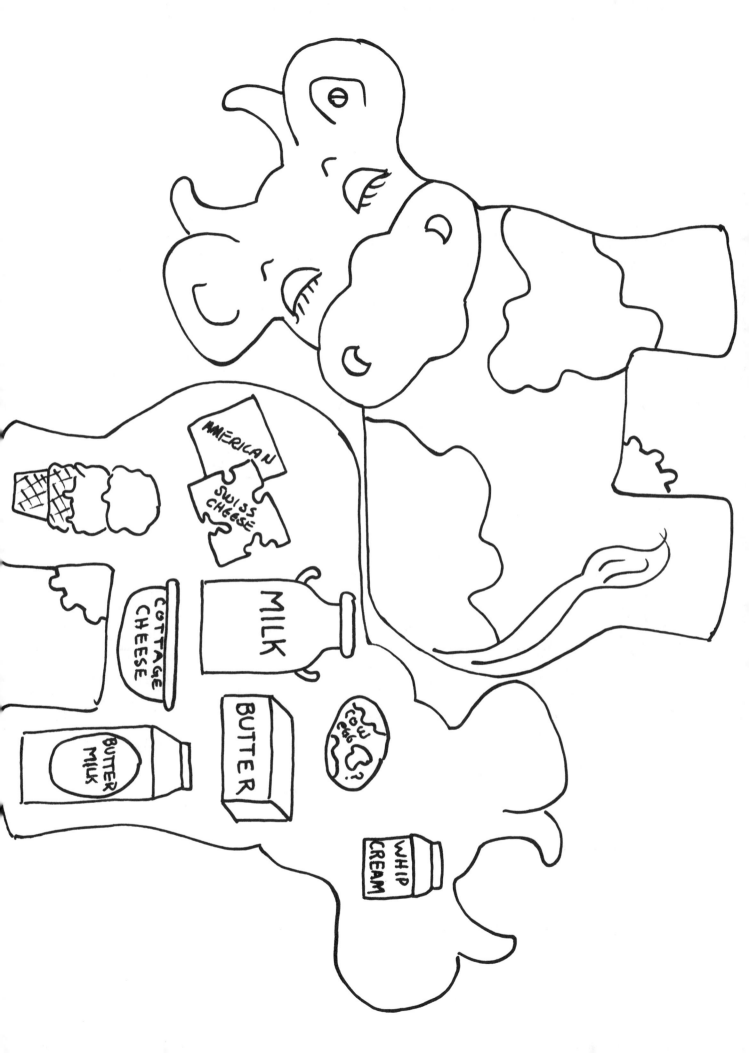

COW PUZZLE — *Painting Directions*

This piece is very special to me, as the cow herself was designed by my eldest daughter Cathi as a locket, and I want to thank her for the design. Thanks honey, Love Ya! Since I have several lockets already I took the liberty of enlarging it, adding a few other things on the inside, and making it into a puzzle for a child. This pattern was especially designed to include in this book. It is darling as a locket though, so feel free to shrink it back down and have a go at it. Instead of making the pieces fit like this one, just leave them loose like the other lockets in the book.

SUPPLIES:

#12 flat   **#5 round**   **10/0 liner**   **tweezers**

Delta Jewelry glaze

Delta clear wood sealer

Sand. Seal and lightly sand again if needed. Be sure to tack before continuing.

Palette: Delta Ceramcoat.

White	**Black**
Tropic Bay	**Drizzle Gray**
Hydrangea	**Crocus**
Yellow	**Silver**
Lt. Ivory	**Butter Yellow**
Nectar	**Antique Gold**
Pink Frosting	**Golden Brown**

White Base coat entire cow. Be sure to do the edges! Now set all but the very top piece aside.

Top piece: Trace and apply pattern with graphite paper.

Black	Her spots are a float of black, or if you prefer you can just paint them a light wash of black. Hooves are black.
Hydrangea	Base her nose (muzzle) inside her ears, and her udder.
Tropic Bay	Wash her eyelids.
Drizzle gray	Float top of ears, across head, under muzzle (on top and bottom), around spots and tail, and where her tummy meets her udder. Base in her horns now.
Black	Float her nostrils with a very light wash of black.

With a 10/0 liner outline her tail, and bring in a few "tail hairs". Paint on her eyebrows, eyelashes and her little mouth. (Don't forget to thin the paint for this.)

Lastly, pull up a few little tiny hairs inside her ears. We wouldn't want any little critters getting in there would we? Set aside to dry.

Center section:

Hydrangea:	Paint top surface only, do not paint inside the holes the puzzle pieces fit into. This will cause the wood to swell, and the pieces will no longer fit!

Puzzle pieces: Freehand patterns on. Base coat each piece as follows:

Swiss cheese	Crocus
Milk can	Silver.
American cheese	Yellow
Cottage cheese	White
Butter	Butter Yellow (what else?)
Buttermilk	Lt. Ivory.
Ice cream cone	Light wash of Golden Brown

Scoops	Nectar and Crocus
Cow Egg	White with Black spots
Whip cream	Lt. Ivory

Of course if you choose to paint your cow a different color, you should paint your egg accordingly. My cow only lays the black and white kind. My youngest granddaughter thought they should be in there because they were a "dairy product". Who was I to argue!

Detail:

Swiss cheese	Float edge of cheese, and edge of each hole with Antique Gold.
American cheese	Float with Butter yellow.
Milk can	Float top and left side of lid, under lid and around left side of can with black.
Whip cream	Float drizzle gray under top "flap" on carton, and under fold of carton.
Butter	Float with Antique Gold on line above the word butter, follow it around on the end of the cube also. When that dries, float down the side of the cube on the right side of the line closest to you.
Buttermilk	Same as whip cream.
Cottage cheese	Float drizzle gray on top edge of lid, and down left side float under lid and down left side of bowl.
Ice-cream cone	Float the criss crosses with Golden Brown, float under bottom scoop, down left side and across line on cone with GB also.
Scoops	Float nectar scoop across top and down left side with Pink Frosting Float Crocus scoop across top and down left side with Antique Gold.

With black and a 10/0 liner or 3/0 technical pen, write the appropriate names on the dairy products according to the pattern suggestions. Finish with Delta clear matte finish when dry.

Allow to dry overnight! This is very important, as you do not want the sections to stick together. Premature assembly will cause them to stick. Insert screw where indicated on ear in the top piece.

FISH BOWL PUZZLE

See color section for full color photograph of completed project.

While I designed this primarily as a puzzle, it would also make a wonderful decoration for the bathroom. It is made out of Corian Tile, with a base of walnut. Corian is a nice material to work with. See Choosing your Wood and Materials chapter for more information.

Blade: # 2 Ultra

Materials: 9"x 8" x 3/4" gray or pink Corian for bowl. (It can also be made of wood.)

10"x 3" x 1" walnut. for base.

Cutting Instructions:

Make a copy of the pattern, and apply it to the Corian with spray glue.

Cut the outside perimeter first. Next , separate the "water" from the "fishbowl". Set each piece aside as soon as you have completed the cut. Next, cut all the puzzle pieces inside the bowl.

Cut each fish out along their outside lines Now make the cuts that break the fish apart.

By doing this, you keep your piece much smoother at the cut edge. This way there are fewer marks visible later on.

Hold the tile a little more firmly than you do with any other blade. The Ultra blade is aggressive and tends to pick the tile up on the tight turns if not held firmly enough.

Cut the base out of the walnut piece. Dado a 3/4" slot down the middle 3/8" deep to accommodate the fishbowl. This can be left plain or routered with your favorite bit. (A beading bit yields a very nice look.)

Finishing directions:

Stand: Sand, tack, and seal with Deltas clear wood sealer, and when dry apply two coats of Delta Clear Satin Varnish. No stain is needed.

Fish Bowl: This is very lovely just left unpainted, but for those of you who would like to add some color , you can do so with Delta Ceramcoat acrylics. Apply the colors of your choice. To keep the paint rather translucent, I painted each section and "blotted" very quickly with a paper towel to remove excess paint. If you want a bright end result, put several coats on until you reach the level of color you like. When dry, use Deltas Jewelry glaze to give it a wonderful water like shine. One coat is adequate.

Alternate version: You can make this into a 3-dimensional piece. The fish segments will slide forward and lock into position, Do not cut any of the Puzzle lines at all, but drill a tiny hole just big enough to enable you to insert the blade through, and make an inside cut on each fish. You will want to tilt the table 3 degrees to the left, and cut in a counter clockwise position. Make sure the table is tilted only when cutting the fish, and square it after each fish is cut. You can now push the fish forward and they will stay locked in that position. If you would prefer the fish to recess, cut in a clockwise direction and they will lock in the reverse position.

See color section for full color photograph of completed project.

This was drawn by my sister Mary Lou, who has more talent in her little finger, than I will ever have in my whole body. (And that would be considerable!) She has hundreds of drawings that she has kept stored away. I wanted to let some of them out! The next three tray puzzles are a result of her artistic work. I have included painting instructions for two of them.

Wood: **8" x 10" x 1/4" Apple ply, or Baltic Birch**

8" x 10" x 1/8" Baltic birch plywood

Refer to general instructions for layout and cutting.

The age of the child you are making this for will determine how large each puzzle piece should be made. For a small child, you may want to cut only one or two pieces apart. Example: His entire body could be left in one piece, his head in another, as well as making some cuts across his legs to separate them from the torso. For a larger child (one that does not put the pieces in his or her mouth), you can cut as many pieces as you like. Example: Cut the hat and ears in one piece. Cut the scarf and neck area in one piece. Cut the arms out separately. Cut the torso and legs out, and last of all his cute little shoes. Remember! You can enlarge any pattern to make it safer for a child.

Sand. Seal and lightly sand again. Tack to remove dust.

Painting directions:
Do these with washes of paint only. Do not apply a heavy concentrate of paint. Washes leave nothing to chip off later.

Brushes: **#12 flat**   **#5 round**   **10/0 liner**

Thin paints with water 3-1 ratio. (3 parts water, 1 part paint)

Remove pieces and basecoat the entire board in DG. Slip slap Straw on floor, and behind feet and legs. Basecoat hat and shoes in Straw. Bear is based in AB. Scarf is CR.

Shirt is Cactus. Overalls are based in W with Cactus and RF stripes alternated.

Inside door frame is AB. Outside frame is CR. With your liner and Crocus bring out some individual pieces of straw. Go in all directions. Float designs on shoes with AB. Laces are Black. Float sleeves and pants with RF. Highlight some of the stripes on his pants in Crocus, and some in Rain Forest. Stitches are Blk. Paint his buckles Crocus. Float RF + Blk. inside buckle on bottom, under flap, around his fly, and under cuff. Float details in ears, and around bear's face in full strength AB. Outline buckles in Black. Do crosshatch pattern on his scarf, and hat with watered down Black. Eyes are Black with White highlights. Float AB all around the inside edge of the door.

Lightly sand all pieces, and tack to remove dust. Apply a coat of Delta Clear satin varnish.

Let dry before putting pieces in.

"DINA " THE LITTLE FARM GIRL.

See color section for full color photograph of completed project.

Refer to general instructions for Tray puzzles.

Supplies

8 1/2″ x 10″ x 1/4″ Apple Plywood, one piece

8 1/2″ x 10″ x 1/8″ Birch ply or door skin, one piece

Yellow wood glue, clamps

Stack and cut both of the pieces at the same time to be sure they are exactly the same size.

Set the bottom piece (the 1/9″ piece) aside. Apply the pattern to the top piece with spray glue, and drill a pilot hole where indicated by arrow to begin your cut. Cut the outside of the girl all the way around, and remove her. Set the rest of the piece to one side.

Now.cut the puzzle in pieces — large or small — depending on the size of the child you are making this for. You may want to cut her head and the tie on her scarf in one piece, her arms, shoulders, hands, back up to her waist, around her other hand and back up to the other shoulder in one piece. Her skirt and basket in one piece, and finally her shoes cut individually. Cut out the skirt, basket, and shoes in one larger piece, if the child is too small to keep her shoes out of its mouth.

If the child is older you can cut as many pieces as you like i.e.: separate arms, feet, etc. I think you have the idea now. The nest and the chickens do not come out, and are only there to add the background interest.

Once you have completed cutting, follow directions for gluing and clamping

Sand. Seal, and lightly sand again before painting. Don't forget to tack.

Painting Directions

She is painted very simply. A good project for the beginner. All the colors are put on in a wash of paint (paint diluted to 3 parts water to one part paint).

Supplies:
Delta clear wood sealer, Delta clear satin varnish

Brushes: **#12 flat.........#5 Round.........#10/0 liner.**

Base Chicken nest in SB with the #12 flat.

Slip slap some SB around chickens, and under nest, then slip slap some Straw, in those same areas.

With the #5 round, base the hens in Candy Bar, and paint their cones in C. Beaks are Blk with White highlights. With the liner, paint CB comma strokes for wings and tail feathers.

With your liner and watered down Straw, paint in individual pieces of hay all over the areas you slip slapped the SB on. Go over it again in several areas with GB, and then with Crocus for the highlights.

Use the # 10 flat and base her skirt in tidepool and float with a light wash of LB. Highlight her skirt with White.

With the #5 round paint the ruffle with White, and highlight with LB.

With your #5 round wash the basket in Straw, the eggs in Palomino. Float the details on the basket with the # 10 brush and AB. Highlight the eggs with a little comma stroke.

Base her blouse in White, and shade with Straw.

That is all you need to do. Leave as is or finish with Deltas Clear varnish.

cut entire section
- out -

cut

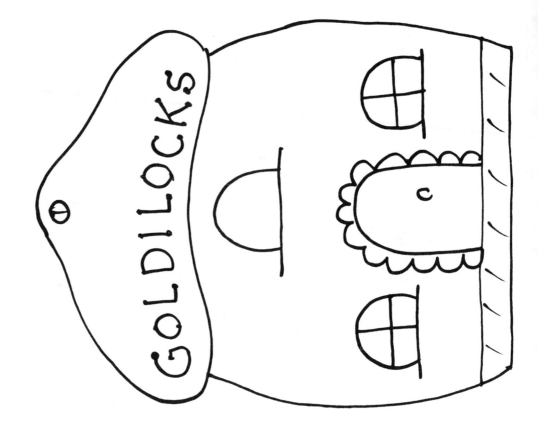

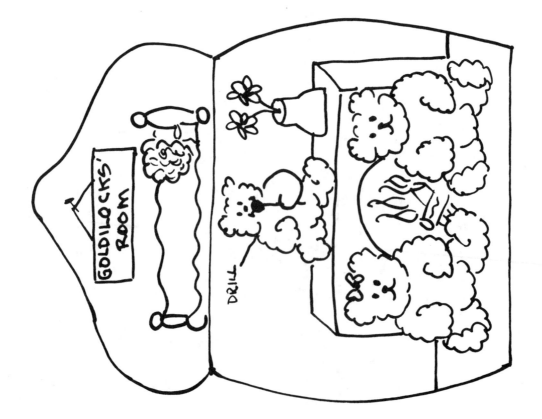

Chapter 8

Lockets and Small Wonders™

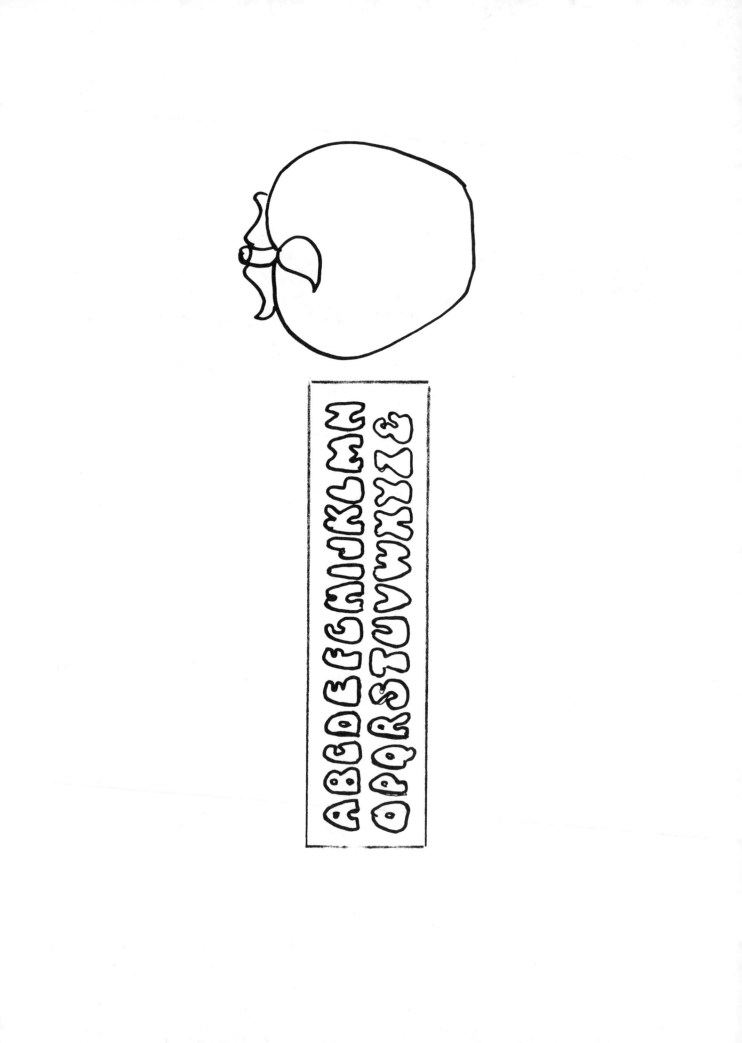

ABCDEFGHIJKLMN
OPQRSTUVWXYZ&

If you would rather not make these tiny little versions, I have included much larger versions of all of these in the Puzzle section. In the larger versions, the pieces are large enough for children to play with safely.

General Directions for All Lockets

APPLE NECKLACE

Since all of the lockets are made the same way, rather than putting specific directions for each one in front of each project, I am going to simplify it by putting the general directions at the beginning of this section. The actual cutting steps are the same for each one, only the wood dimensions will vary. (Unless otherwise stipulated.) Pieces of 4" square woods will work for any of the pieces, giving you adequate room to hold onto the piece while cutting.

For each necklace you will need the following wood and hardware supplies:

Two 4"x 4" x 1/8" pieces of Baltic birch plywood. (Birch doorskin will also work).

One 4"x 4" x 3/16" piece of maple birch, or similar hardwood.

One 2" x 5" x 5/32 piece of maple or birch or similar hard wood*. (This is the stock the small pieces are cut from , and it must be thinner than the center section. If it is not, a heavy coat of paint plus the final glaze will make the price too thick for the lid to swivel closed properly.) If you do not have a planer, simply sand the 3/16" on both sides on a belt sander. Sand off approximately 1/32". This will be adequate to compensate for the painting.

You will also need:

#3 double tooth scroll saw blades	#2 brass wood screw*
a hand drill and 1/8″ drill bit.	#217 1/2 brass screw eye.*
spray glue	yellow wood glue
spring clothespins	tiny screw driver
18″ of rat tail cord or ribbon	*Source page

Cutting Instructions

Make 2 copies of all of the patterns. Install a #3 blade.

Sandwich the two pieces of the precut Baltic birch ply-wood, on each side of the piece of maple, being very sure the smooth sides are facing front and back. Tape them together with 1/4″ masking tape . **(photo # 29)** Apply the pattern you will be cutting to the top piece with spray glue. **(photo #30)**.

Cut the pattern out, holding the wood firmly on each side **(photo #31)** remove the tape, and set the two thin pieces of Baltic birch aside.

Apply the inside pattern to the piece of maple you just cut out. **(photo #32)** Drill a tiny hole in the center of the piece that is to be removed and insert the top of the blade through the hole from the bottom of the wood piece. **(photo #33)** Re-insert the blade into the blade clamp, **(photo # 34)** tension the machine and you are ready to cut. Follow the line around and remove this piece and discard. **(photo #35)**

Note: if the hole in your table is large enough for the small pieces to fall through— make an overlay for the table, as described earlier in the Scroll Saw Basics chapter. If you are having trouble with the little pieces breaking loose just as you finish the cut, place a fingernail over the tiny piece as you finish off. **(photo #36)** This will eliminate the problem. (For those of you who do not have long nails, place your index finger of your non- dominant hand behind the blade as close as possible!)

Apply pattern for small pieces to the 2″ x 5″ x 5/32″ piece of wood. **(Photo #36 again)** (this is the largest piece you will

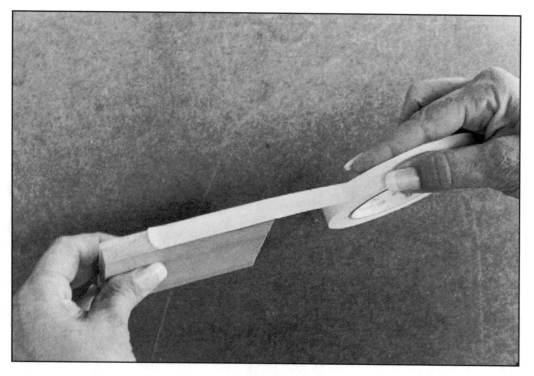

Photo #29   *Assembling the sandwich of plywood-maple-plywood and taping around edges with masking tape prior to stack-cutting.*

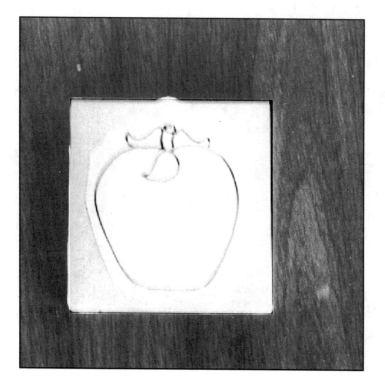

Photo #30   *Spray glue the pattern to the top of the sandwiched woods.*

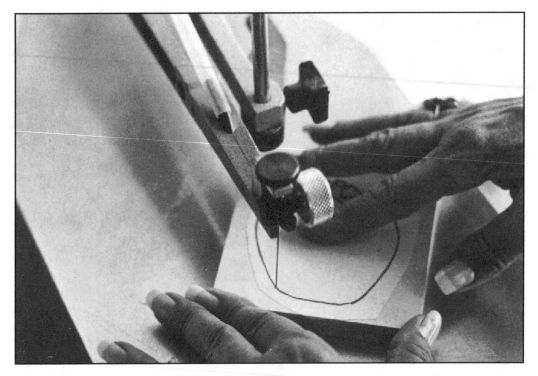

Photo #31   *Your first cut is along the perimeter of the pattern. Notice how hands are positioned for safety and accuracy.*

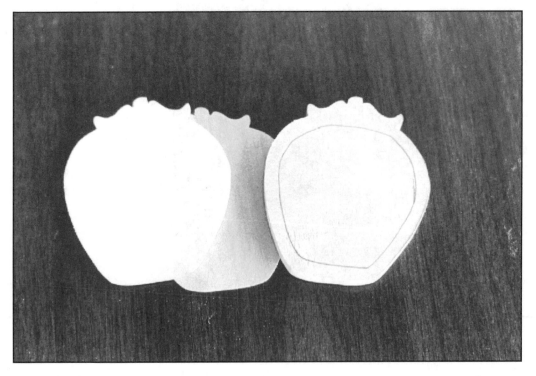

Photo #32   *Inside pattern applied to maple center and pilot hole drilled.*

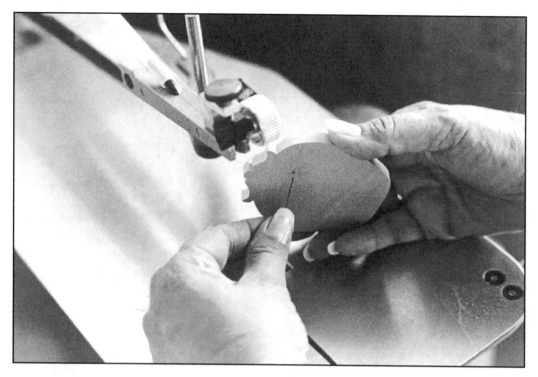

Photo #33   *Threading blade through bottom of wood in preparation for the inside cut.*

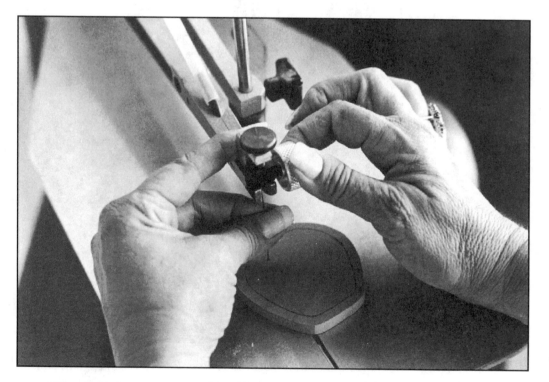

Photo #34   *Re-attaching blade in upper blade clamp. Note position of fingers during this operation.*

Photo #35   *Interior cut made-creating the hollow section of each locket. Discard this core-it will not be needed.*

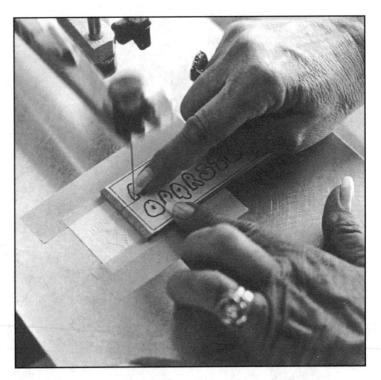

Photo #36   *Apply Apple Alphabet to strip of 5/32" alder and cut out. Note use of temporary business card overlay necessary when cutting these small piece. My extra-length fingernails come in very handy at this stage to hold down small pieces to finish cuts.*

be needing for any of the lockets). Please bear in mind the size of the wood is approximate. You can get by using a smaller piece of wood, but if you are new to sawing this small, it would be better for you to use my specifications. Carefully cut all pieces out and set aside.

Sanding: I use an emery board to sand the entire piece. An excellent source for these is a beauty supply house. Ask for the emery boards the women use for acrylic nails. Get the black padded ones. They last forever! While your there you might also ask for sanding blocks used on nails. They are the finest fine sanding blocks I have ever found anywhere, and will cost far less than what tool stores normally charge.

Assembly Instructions:

Apply a thin line of yellow wood glue to the back of the center section. **(Photo #37)** Line up with the bottom section, so that all edges are even. Squeeze together and wipe any glue that oozes out on the sides or in the "hole" with a damp cloth . Clamp with clothespin clamps **(photo #38)**. Clean any excess glue with a wet Q-tip. When dry, insert small pieces. **(Photo # 39)** Drill the tiny holes you will need to insert the screw, and screw eye where indicated by arrows.

If you want to cut two of these pieces out at a time you can easily do so. Stack all of the layers of wood needed for two necklaces, (6 layers) and use a #5 blade to cut them. Then stack two pieces of the thinner hardwood together and cut the tiny pieces out in duplicate .

If you are going to be making more than two, you can stack the thinner wood four pieces deep, and cut out many more at once. I only cut two of the main pieces out at a time, but since I make so many of the lockets, I cut out four of the inside pieces at time, and store them in a small blue metal storage cabinets with drawers . You can buy this type of cabinet at any hardware or discount store. They are great for storing small pieces of wood and hardware as well.

Note: If you are burning your maple, change the blade...it's dull. Maple dulls your blades rapidly!

Painting Instructions

When painting the small pieces, put a piece of masking tape around your index finger on your non-dominant hand with the sticky side out. Place the little pieces on the tape, and paint away.

Since this locket uses only four different colors, I am not including specific painting directions. But here are a few basic ideas. Paint the entire Apple Red (inside, outside and the edges and the back) paint the leaf Green and the stem Brown. Paint the alphabet Black When dry take each letter and sand it lightly to take the paint off of the edges. This makes the letters stand out better.

PRIMITIVE ARK PUZZLE

This pattern was adapted from a piece by Gus Steufureac of Quality Woodcrafters.

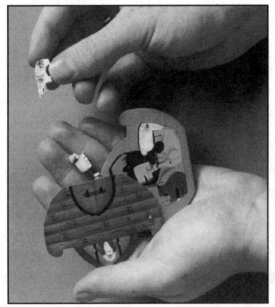

Refer to general locket instructions for cutting until you are ready to cut the "inside" section out. Then refer to the special instructions below.

Since these pieces fit back in puzzle fashion rather than loosely, the small pieces will be cut from the little section that you remove. Because of this, make sure that you drill the hole right at the arrow, rather than just anywhere as in the other lockets. Once you have the hole drilled, cut the entire outside edge of the

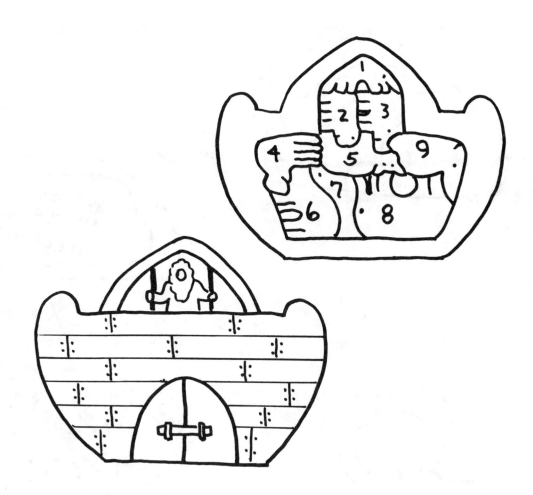

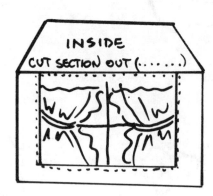

INSIDE
CUT SECTION OUT (.......)

CUT OUT ENTIRE SECTION

X = drill

INSIDE

CUT OUT THIS AREA

FRONT

↑ = screw eye
X = screw for swivel

Cut out of center

inside out. Cut each piece loose and set aside until you have them all cut out. Make a couple of copies of this, or you will never get them back in! Continue as in general directions for gluing and clamping.

Painting Directions

Brushes & Supplies

#12 flat	#5 round	10/0 liner	tweezers
Delta clear wood sealer		Delta Jewelry glaze	
Yellow wood glue		spring clothespins.	

Sand, seal with Delta clear wood sealer and lightly sand again if needed. Transfer pattern with graphite paper to the top piece. I believe you will find it almost as easy to freehand the pattern onto the small pieces as you will to try to line them up well enough to trace.

Palette: Delta Ceramcoat

Golden Brown	**Lichen Gray**
Rain Forest	**Antique Gold**
Luscious Lemon	**Burnt Umber**
Fleshtone	**Burnt Sienna**
White	**Black**

Base entire ark in GB.

Apply pattern to front of ark. Base window in LL.

Base Noah as follows:

Face and hands FT...Hair...WH...Robe RF...Float around face next to hairline with BU (very lightly). With a mix of RF and Blk (diluted 4-1), float on robe across upper arms, under beard and under arms. Float under mustache.

Paint columns next to Noah Blk. Float planks on ark, around window, and inside door with BU. Paint "wrought iron" around door blk, as well as the braces on the door. Paint wood plank in braces BU, and detail some wood grain in Blk with 10/0 liner.

Float BU down center of door. Add "nails" on ark with a stylus and Blk. To finish Noah off take your 10/0 liner and thin out some White. Pull some hair out from both his hair and his beard to make him look at bit tattered. (This was before men started using blow dryers and hair spray you know!) Make him look as if he is in need of some grooming.

Animals:

Since these are rather unusual shapes, it is hard to call some of them by name. I have decided to use the paint by number system to avoid any confusion here.

#1. Burnt sienna

#2. Base in W. Ears and nose are Blk. Float lightly with B.

#3. WH + BS (ratio 3-1). Float details with Blk.

#4. Antique Gold.

#5   Base W. With dry brush, give her some spots. Outline her ears in Blk. Hooves are B. Her udders and muzzle are WH+BS (ratio 4-1).

#6. Burnt umber.

#7. Base RF with a BS float on her tummy. Her beak is AG.

#8. Lichen gray with float of Blk.

#9. Base W...spots are W+B (ratio 4-1). Nose is BS+W (ratio 1-4). Float the same mixture in the center of her ear. Liner her whiskers in B.All hooves are Blk, as are all eyes and noses (except bunny).

Finish with Jewelry glaze, allow to dry, and add hardware. Do not put animals inside ark until very very dry, or they may never come out again!

See color section for full color photograph of this project.

Refer to general cutting directions for lockets.

Painting Directions

Brushes & supplies
#12 flat   #5 round
10/0 liner tweezers
Delta clear wood sealer
Delta Jewelry glaze

Sand. Seal with Delta clear wood sealer. Lightly sand again if needed. Transfer pattern with graphite paper to the top piece. I believe you will find it almost as easy to freehand the pattern onto the small pieces as you will to try to line them up well enough to trace.

Pallete: Delta Ceramcoat

Ivory	*Bright Yellow*
Stoneware Blue	*Green Sea*
Nightfall	*Forest Green*
Black	*Flesh Tone*
Mocha	

Presentation:

Sand, tack, and seal. When dry, base coat with ivory.

Painting the House

Apply pattern. Dampen front of house with plain water, and apply a soft wash of SB. With a clean brush and a little water remove almost all of the paint in the windows.

Base planters, and roof in SB.

Base shutters in NF.

Base welcome sign in Ivory.

Base windows inside and out with a wash of BY.

Base trees and plants in window boxes in FG.

Float tiles on roof in NF.

With a very light wash of SB, float top and left side of windows and around left side of door.

On the inside window, where the curtains are, paint the panes of the window with your liner and black. Set aside.

Outline all the details on the front of the house with the same liner and black. (Or use the pen.) When you outline the tiles, keep it loose while looking at photograph of finished project. Don't paint a solid line — break it up.

Now go back to the inside window again. Float the curtains in white. These need to be heavy enough to see the detail of the folds and ruffle but light enough to be sheer. Float next to the ruffle with NF to make it stand out. Paint the area around the outside of the window of the middle portion in SB. (It will make the curtains stand out more.)

With the smallest end of your stylist, SB and BY, dot some flowers on your flower boxes. You may even choose to add some red flowers. Any shade will do. With GS, stipple some highlights on the shrubbery.

Painting the Children

Base skin areas in Fleshtone. Because they are so small, I will leave the choice of clothing colors up to you (refer to color section). Use some of the colors on the palette to balance things off. All kids have Mocha hair, and Black shoes. Their faces are shaded with a light wash of Mocha. Their eyes are dotted black with a stylus. A white high-light is added when dry.

Brush the Jewelry Glaze over each piece and allow to dry overnight before assembly.

EASTER BUNNY NECKLACE © 1991

Refer to general cutting directions for lockets.

See color section for a full color photograph of this project.

Painting Directions:

Brushes & supplies:

    #12 flat   #5 round   10/0 liner   1/4" deersfoot

    tweezers   Delta clear wood sealer

    Delta Jewelry glaze

Sand, seal , and lightly sand again if needed. Transfer pattern with graphite paper to the top piece AFTER BASECOATING. I believe you will find it almost as easy to freehand the pattern onto the small pieces as you will to try to line them up well enough to trace.

Palette: Delta Ceramcoat

Ivory	***Deep River***
Hydrangea	***Black***
Drizzle Gray	***Liberty Blue***
Rain Forest	***Bright Red***
Bright Yellow	***White***

Painting:

Base coat all bunnies with Ivory. Basecoat all eggs with White. Lightly sand. Apply pattern.

Float bunnies with Drizzle Gray. Float around wreath also. Float the spots on the Mama bunny with a very light wash of Drizzle Gray. With Hydrangea , base portion of ears where indicated, paint nose and pitty-pat cheek. Her eye is lined in Black, and her eye should be Hydrangea, but you may paint it Black if preferred.

Wreath: Stipple Rain Forest in wreath area. Keep it light, and loose. With small stylus apply Bright Yellow flowers, then White, and finally a few Bright Red. Pull a few leaves out with Deep River. Don't over do the leaves - just a few for added color.

As a final touch, outline the spots with your 10/0 liner and a light wash of black. Make a few swirls on the tail. Paint the "toes".

Eggs: Since they are so small, you may decorate them to your liking. We have all done this at least once in our lives I'm sure.

Babies: Add dots for eyes. If you feel innovative, you may want to add little bows around their necks with some of the colors in the palette*. Get loose! Have fun!

Paint the "hole" with Rain Forest. Allow to dry, and finish the entire piece with Deltas' Jewelry glaze. Allow to dry overnight. Insert screw eye and screw.

TEDDY BEAR AND BABIES

Refer to general locket directions for cutting.

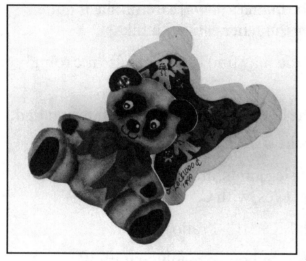

Supplies Needed:

Stylus #10 Flat   #5 Round   10/0 Liner

Delta clear wood sealer   Delta Jewelry Glaze

Palette: Delta Ceramcoat
White
Black
Charcoal
Bright Red
Brown

Preparation

Sand and tack to remove any dust. Seal with Deltas clear wood sealer.

Painting

Use the #10 flat except on the tiny bears, use #5 round.

Base coat entire bear W. Don't forget the babies! Base coat some White, some Black, and some Brown. Your choice. If you are really energetic you can paint them to look like "mama", (little pandas).

Allow to dry completely. Lightly sand with a piece of crumpled up brown paper bag.

Paint the pads of the mama's paws (careful, she is quite ticklish!) around her eyes, and her ears with Blk.

Base her bow BR. You may find it easier to use the round brush for this.

With liner, paint the bows on the teddys in White and Red.

SHADING: (Use the # 10 flat for all shading.)

Float around teddys leg joints, around her ankles, under her bow, and around her eyes, with C.

Float her bow with BR + B (3-1 ratio)

Do a reverse float on her bow to highlight with W.

Put a dot of B in her eye as indicated, and highlight with a small dot of White. Dot her nose with W.

With a 10/0 liner paint her mouth in B. Paint her little nose with #5 round and Blk. When dry, sand again with paper bag.

Final Touches

Put one or two coats of Deltas' Jewelry glaze on all the pieces, allowing them to dry between coats. You might find you only need one, as this dries to a lovely shine with just one coat.

Please do not assemble until you have allowed it to dry overnight.

Insert both screws, insert a rat tail cord and you are ready to wear this adorable necklace.

TEDDY PIN

Refer to general cutting directions for lockets. This piece is different in that there are no tiny pieces to be cut. The center section is for a "Love note," reminder, or a tiny treasure.

Painting Directions

Brushes & supplies

#12 flat   #5 round   10/0 liner.   Delta Jewelry glaze Delta clear wood sealer.   Pin Back.

Sand, seal and lightly sand again if needed. Transfer pattern with graphite paper to the top piece.

Palette: Delta Ceramcoat

Napthol Crimson

Spice Brown

Black

White

Territorial Beige

BEAR: Base entire piece in SB except for the "hole." Apply pattern.

Float the back of his head, inside ear, back of tummy area, under arm, back of arm, back leg, inside arm, next to nose, pad on foot, and mouth next to finger, with SB + B. Paint nose, and space between hand and neck B.

Float top of ear, tummy, left side of arm, top of front leg, and down left side of head seam with W. With NC lightly "blush" his cheeks.

Base the hole in W. When dry apply Dolly Parton hearts to the white section with NC.

BOW: Base in NC. Float where indicated on photo with B + NC. Apply dots with small end of stylus. When dry, add a reverse float of W. for bow highlights.

Paint eye area in W, and dot pupil with black. With a 10/0 liner, or a 3x0 tech pen apply his stitching, and outline his eye. (Only half the eye is outlined.) Allow to dry completely.

When piece is dry, finish with Delta Jewelry glaze. Do not put anything inside until it dries overnight.

This can be made into a locket as well. Simply follow the directions for any one of the other lockets for inserting screw eye.

Thought: This would be darling when enlarged and used as a treasure box. I have included an enlargement in the Pattern Treasury chapter for just that purpose. If you increase the thickness of the wood, you must use a larger screw.

3 BEARS LOCKET

See color section for a full color photograph of this finished project.

This piece is cut the same way as the other lockets under General directions, with the following exceptions. The three bears are done like the "tray puzzles" and fit in the house puzzle style. For this necklace you will be using the center section to cut the Bears out of rather than using a larger piece of wood. After you have finished cutting the outside perimeter, set the two thin sections aside. Apply the pattern to the remaining section, drill a tiny hole where indicated on pattern for each bear, insert the blade from the bottom and cut the bears out carefully. Set them aside, and continue gluing according to general locket directions.Re-apply the pattern to the front and mark the upstairs window. Drill a tiny hole and cut out.

CUT ENTIRE SECTION OUT.

Cookies

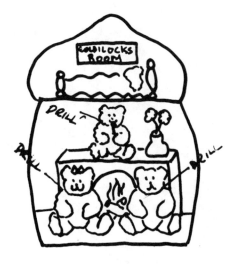

GOLDILOCKS ROOM

DRILL

DRILL

DRILL

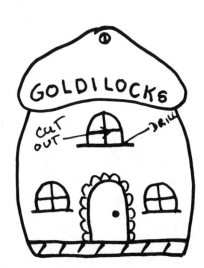

GOLDILOCKS

CUT OUT

DRILL

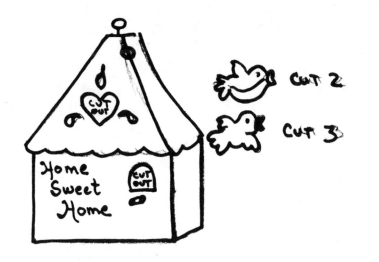

CUT OUT

Home Sweet Home

CUT OUT

CUT 2

CUT 3

Painting Instructions

Other supplies needed.

#12 flat   #5 round   10/0 liner   tweezers

Delta Jewelry glaze   Yellow wood

glue   spring clothes pins   Stylus

Sand. Seal with Delta clear wood sealer and lightly sand again if needed. Transfer pattern with graphite paper to the top piece. I believe you will find it almost as easy to freehand the pattern onto the small pieces as you will to try to line them up well enough to trace.

Inside the house:

Wash walls with FG Paint carpet with full strength FG.

Wash fireplace with BR and the inside of the Fireplace in B.

The wall paper optional, and needs to be freehanded on. It is painted with your liner in FG and W stripes. Float FG around the entire fireplace and all the way across the house under the bed area.

Float B to form the details on the fireplace.

The vase is painted Y with a float of AB for shading. The stems on the flowers are LG with Y liner on one side. The flowers are five little dots forming a circle in CR with W dot centers.

Logs in fireplace are AB with B at base of logs. Flame is Y with CR streaks.

Goldilocks bedspread is TP with CB float. Pillow and dust ruffle are W with Black liner to outline. Bed posts areAB.

Sign is W with B lettering.

Bears: Base in AB. Stipple with dry deersfoot brush or scruffy brush in AB + W. Their noses and eyes are Black dots.

Outside of House:
Base house in SS Base Roof, shutters and door in TP.

Base windows in C. Base curtains in W Front porch is SB.

Details:
Float CB around roof, under roof, on top of windows and door at base of house and half way around windows starting at left bottom side and ending on the knife edge of your brush at the top of the window. With B and liner, paint windowpanes. Be sure to water your paint down for liner work.

With CB and liner outline shutters.

Float BU on porch for individual boards. and float under house now too.

Stipple LG on flower boxes, and add dots of C and W for flowers.

Seal when dry with Jewelry glaze, and allow to dry overnight before putting the piece together.

Add screws and rat tail cord and your locket is ready to wear or give away.

The cutting directions for this are the same as the other lockets with one exception. The little heart windows are cut out by drilling a hole, inserting the top of the blade through the bottom and re inserting the blade back into the upper blade clamp (as in fretwork). Cut these out after you have separated the three pieces but before you glue the sections together.

Painting Directions

#12 flat   **#5 round**   **10/0 liner** **tweezers**

Delta Jewelry glaze   **Yellow wood**

glue   **spring clothes pins**   **Stylus.**

Sand. Seal with Delta clear wood sealer, and lightly sand again if needed. Transfer pattern with graphite paper to the top piece. I believe you will find it almost as easy to freehand the pattern onto the small pieces as you will to try to line them up well enough to trace.

Palette: Delta Ceramcoat

Copen Blue	*Crimson Red*
White	*Custard*
Palomino	*Autumn Brown*
	Black

Base the birds in CB Float their little tummies with CR. Their beaks are C and their eyes are

B. Base the heart inside the birdhouse in CR.

Base the outside in P. Float side of house and roof line with AB. (See photo)

Paint the inside of the house (where the birds go) Black.

Perch in front of window is AB outlined with B. (this may be omitted)

Lettering is done with liner in B.

With your liner, make white comma strokes around the edge of the house.

Red comma strokes around the little heart window.

With your stylus or tip of paint brush handle that you have sharpened in a pencil sharpener, make a Dolly Parton heart. (Dolly Parton heart is made by placing two dots of paint side by side and pulling a tail from the middle of them with your liner to make the tail on the heart.)

Finish when dry with Delta Jewelry glaze. Allow to dry overnight before putting the birds in the house.

COOKIE JAR LOCKET:

See color section for full color photograph of this completed project.

Follow general locket directions for cutting.

Painting Directions

Brushes needed: **#12 flat #5 round 10/0 liner.**

Palette: Delta Ceramcoat	
Golden Brown	***White***
Autumn Brown	***Candy Bar***
Tomato Spice	***Tidepool***
Chocolate Brown	

Sand. Seal with Delta clear wood sealer, and lightly sand again if needed. Transfer pattern with graphite paper to the top piece. I believe you will find it almost as easy to freehand the pattern onto the small pieces as you will to try to line them up well enough to trace.

Procedure:

With a #12 flat base the lid of the cookie jar in Golden Brown. Base the jar itself in White.

Base the tiny gingerbread men in Golden Brown. Don't forget the edges of the little guys.

Base the handle on the lid in White.

Float Autumn Brown around all of the gingerbread men, and the jar lid with your #12 flat brush.

With a 10/0 liner and White, do the "icing" on the gingerbread men. Some of them get a little heart for their buttons, and the others get a little raisin. The heart is done with the stylus, and Tomato Spice, and the raisins are done with the tip of your #5 round and Candy Bar.

Give the little guys a rest now, and with your flat brush, float a very light wash of Tidepool under the lid of the jar, and down the left side. With your liner and a that same wash of Tidepool paint a few streaks on the jar itself in a curve to give it a round look.

With your stylus, make chocolate chips on the lid with Chocolate Brown (of course!)

Finish by writing Cookies on the jar with your liner and Candy Bar.

Finish all pieces with Deltas Jewelry glaze, and when dry attach hardware.

Chapter 9

Fretwork Projects

FRETWORK PROJECTS

Since there are a number of trivet sets in this book, I am giving the actual cutting and assembly directions here at the beginning.

All trivets and coasters are cut the same way, only the dimensions of the wood will be changed

You may also wish to experiment with Corian Tile (see Materials Chapter). This is a counter top material. It requires no finish and will handle very hot dishes without scorching.

Materials List:

Proper wood type and size for each pattern (All trivets are made from 1/2″ wood, all coasters 1/4″ wood)

3/4″ hardwood "Buttons"

1/32″ drill bit.

#3 double tooth blade, or a #5 reverse tooth blade

spray glue

Hand sander or equivalent with very fine sanding paper.

Yellow wood glue

Delta Ceramcoat paints

Cutting Instructions:

Cut wood to proper size for project. Cut the outside perimeter out last.

Make copy of pattern for future use. Spray glue pattern onto the back of the wood. Apply pattern to wood.

Drill a pilot hole wherever there is wood to be removed. (indicated by black area and/or an x)

Refer to photographs in general directions of Lockets chapter if necessary. These inside cuts are done in the same way.

Install your blade in the bottom clamp only of your saw, and put the top of the blade through one of the holes you just drilled. Re-attach the blade to the top clamp in your machine and tighten your tension according to manufacturers directions. Cut this area out. Loosen your tension, remove blade from upper clamp, re-insert through another hole, re-attach into upper clamp, and re-tension your machine.

Repeat these steps until you have finished removing all blackened areas and areas marked with an X.

If you dread doing Fretwork because of the trouble and time it takes, you may want to consider a special Fretwork knob available for some machines.

To see clamping device in place on machine refer to photo #23 in locket chapter.

I would not recommend cutting the entire piece out with one blade. Although, it can be done if you are very accomplished and own a top quality saw. If you are burning the wood change blades. Your finished product will be far more pleasing to the eye if the cuts are clean and precise.

Hint: If you are having trouble following the outside circular pattern, I suggest you cut just outside the line, and when finished take the piece to a belt sander and sand down to the line. You will not have to do this once you have become quite proficient on the scroll saw.

Sand on both sides with your hand sander.

Glue the button feet on the bottom with yellow wood glue. Allow to dry.

Since coasters are made from thinner material, you can stack cut these two at a time.

Painting directions will follow those projects that are painted.

Idea! Experiment with different types of woods when

making these. Walnut is lovely if you choose not to paint the finished item. Mahogany can a bit stringy at times although it finishes nicely. If hardwoods are difficult to find in your area or are prohibitive in price, you may want to find some Apple Plywood. It really is beautiful when cut out and stained. The multiple woods used to form the ply stain different shades. This gives a lovely unique look to your project.

If you are not going to paint these, I recommend using a good polyurethane finish. It will accept heat and water without damaging the wood.

If you are not going to use them for very hot pans, you can get away with using Delta Jewelry Glaze, or any clear glaze finish. It puts a high gloss finish on the piece and brings out the beauty of the grain.

Want to design your own trivets and coasters? Take a square piece of paper about the size you want the finished trivet to be. Now fold it into quarters. With a pair of sharp scissors start cutting little nips and designs out. Gently unfold occasionally, to see what you have created, and add a few more cuts here and there where needed.

When finished, choose the correct size piece of wood, apply the paper and cut!

Bet you didn't realize how creative you could be - did you! If you create an incredible design send me a copy. Be sure to send me a letter along with it, giving me permission to use it in my next book. (Giving you full credit of course!)

BUTTERFLY TRIVET & COASTER SET.

See color section for a full color photograph of the completed project.

Wood:
8 1/2x 8 1/2 x 1/2" Oak. for Trivet

5" x 5" x 1/4" for Coasters. Four pieces

needed this size.

Stack the coasters 2 deep, secure with tape, drill and cut. If you are an advanced cutter you can stack all four coasters and cut them all at one time. For all other cutting instructions, please refer to General directions for trivet and coaster cutting and assembly directions.

Brushes:
   #12 flat   #5 round   10/0 liner.

Other supplies:
   Delta clear wood sealer Delta Jewelry glaze

   3x0 Technical pen and ink. (optional)

   Graphite paper   Stylus   Tracing paper

Palette: Delta Ceramcoat

Antique Rose	**Dark Forest**
Cactus	**Brown Iron Oxide**
Charcoal	**Crocus**
Black	**Prussian Blue**
Phalo Green	**Silver**
Bright Yellow	**Maroon**
	Yellow

Begin by sanding the piece thoroughly, Make sure it is smooth and lint free before you seal.

Seal with clear wood sealer. and allow to dry. Sand very lightly with a brown paper bag which has been crumpled up.

Assemble your painting supplies.
   Water bin, paper towels, Q-tips, (they are great for erasing any painting goofs that you may make) your brushes, paints, and what ever else you think you may need.

Hearts & Flowers

Hearts & Diamonds

Hearts & Roses

Since the coasters are smaller, you may want to start with them. Directions are the same for both.

Trace your pattern and line it up with the cut piece. Hold it very tightly while you slip a small piece of graphite paper under the tracing paper. With a stylus go over all the pattern lines. Before you trace over every one, do just a little and carefully lift the paper up to make sure it is taking. If it isn't, make sure you have the shiny side down.

With your 10/0 liner, or the 3x0 technical pen and thinned black paint (for technical pens use the black ink that comes with them.) Outline all inside pattern lines. It is not necessary to outline the cut edges.

With your #12 flat apply a thin wash of AR. to the flowers (use #5 round for smaller areas.)

Centers of flowers are full strength Cactus

Wash the leaves in DF.

Wash branches in BIO.

Wash top of butterfly wings with Charcoal, and bottom in Crocus.

Detail: All floating is done with the #12 Flat.

Float flower petals with Maroon on one side of each petal, and with White on the opposite side.

Stipple the centers with a mixture of BIO. and Y, and then put in a few Blk. dots. Re-ink center of flower with uneven lines.

Leaves are floated in Ph. G. on the right side.

Branch is floated with full strength BIO. With your pen or 10/0 liner, draw a knothole in the branch, and a few lines here and there, to simulate wood.

The Butterfly is detailed as follows: Float over black areas with Pr. Blue, and then when dry with Ph. Green..

Float over Crocus with Br. Yellow. then with Yellow.

Paint dots Silver. and float them with Ph. Green. Outline with black liner if needed.

Allow to completely dry and finish with Delta's Jewelry glaze. If you do not wish it to shine, finish with a clear matte finish. These finishes are not meant for hot pots and pans, but are acceptable for cold to warm plates.

HEARTS AND FLOWERS FRETWORK DESIGN

I would like to thank Newell Hubbard for taking time out of his busy schedule to cut this and the following trivet for me.

Wood: **8½"x 8½" x 1/2" oak or walnut**

Blade: **#5 reverse tooth**

HEARTS AND DIAMONDS FRETWORK DESIGN

Wood: **9"x 9"x 1/2" Birch or other hardwood**

Blade: **#5 Reverse tooth**

HEARTS AND ROSES FRETWORK DESIGN

Wood: **8"x 8"x 1/2" Dark Walnut**

Blade: **#5 doubletooth**

This is beautiful when made from dark walnut !

NORMANDY FRETWORK DESIGN

Wood: 10″ x 10″ x 1/2″ Hardwood.
             (Oak, Birch, Walnut)

Blade: #5 reverse tooth.

"MORNING" FRETWORK DESIGN

Blade: #5 reverse tooth

Wood: 10″ x 10″ x 1/2″ hardwood.

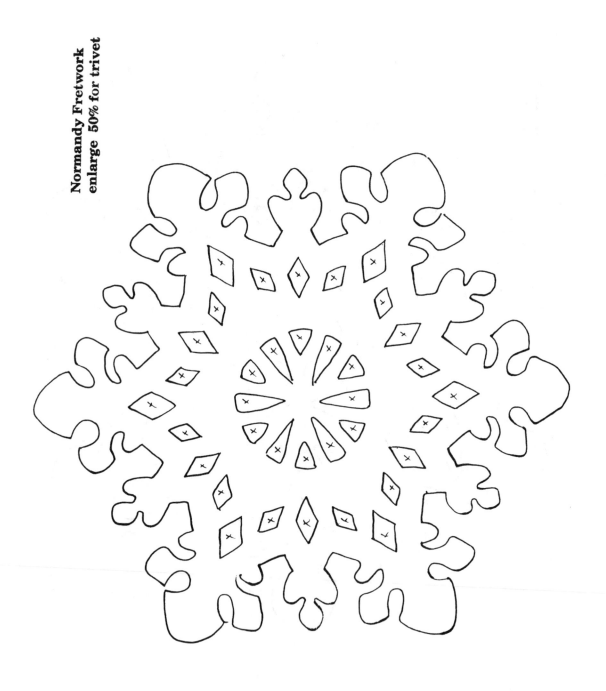

Chapter 10

Collapsible Baskets

COLLAPSIBLE BASKETS

Baskets are a fun challenge for scroll saw woodcrafters. The actual basket is made with one long continuous cut. The basket then "pops" out and locks into place!

Baskets look so interesting and intriguing - they are real show-stoppers.

The above basket was especially designed for this book by Rick Longabaugh of The Berry Basket in Centralia, Washington. Consult the sources page for Rick's address to send for a catalog of more plans and materials.

The directions and patterns that follow are ©1991 by The Berry Basket and are used with permission.

General Basket Instructions

Materials

Scrollsaw blades - #7 to cut the pattern and
  #9 to cut the basket rungs
3/4 " Hardwood
Spray adhesive
Oil (Min-Wax, Danish or Tung)
Drill bits - 1/16" and 1/8"

Countersink - 1/4" to 3/8"
Router bit - 1/4" roundover
Small drum or pad sander
6/32 Machine screws: flathead ▷〰〰〰 or
  roundhead ⊖〰〰〰
or #6 Wood screws: flathead ▷〰〰 or
  roundhead ⊖〰〰

Instructions

To use these patterns most effectively, we suggest making photo copies of the pattern you wish to cut out. An advantage to the copier is that you can enlarge or reduce the pattern to fit the size wood you choose to use. Use a spray adhesive to adhere the pattern to the wood. Spray adhesives can be purchased at most arts & crafts, photography, and department stores. Pay special attention to purchase one that states "temporary bond" or "repositionable". Lightly spray the back of the pattern, not the wood, then position the pattern onto the work piece.

Two factors will determine how deep the basket will fold out, the thickness of the blade, and the bevel of the table when cutting. A thicker blade produces a deeper basket, as does the 4° bevel over the 5°. Therefore, we recommend practicing with an inexpensive grade of wood until you determine the proper bevel for the thickness of the blade you are using. In the materials listed above we have recommended 2 different scrollsaw blade sizes. We suggest using the #7 blade to cut the pattern with, and the #9 blade to cut the basket rungs. The following chart gives the approximate bevels for most #9 blades. However keep in mind that different brands of blades will vary in thickness, which will then affect how deep the basket will fold out. To determine the bevels in the chart below, a #9 blade with the following specs was used: width .053, thickness .018 and TPI 11.5.

To measure the circle or oval measure at the basket's pivot points from one dotted line on the pattern to the other (see example at right). Find the size of the circle, oval,   (to the nearest 1/2") on the chart below to give you the proper bevel. Keep in mind that if you reduce or enlarge the pattern you will need to adjust the bevel accordingly.

Bevel Chart

Circle	4 1/2"	5"	5 1/2"	6"	6 1/2"	7"
bevel	6°	5 1/2°	5°	4 1/2°	4°	3 1/2°
Oval	5"	5 1/2"	6"	6 1/2"	7"	7 1/2"
bevel	7°	6 1/2°	6°	5 1/2°	5 °	4 1/2°

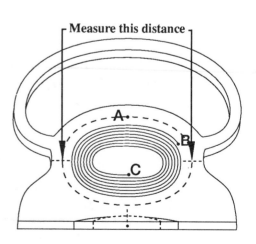

Measure this distance

The following hardwoods are good choices for making the baskets: ash, maple - curly and birdseye, walnut - eastern and curly, flaming birch, mahogany - cuban and ribbon, curly hickory, curly cherry, and red oak. Please keep in mind, however, that this is not a complete list of the beautiful hardwoods available.

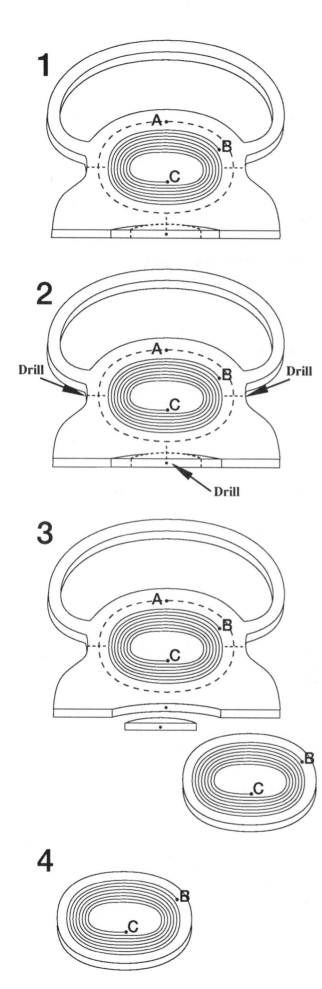

Basket Instructions

Step 1 Adhere pattern to work piece. Cut outer shape and design of basket.

Step 2 Mark the drill points using a hammer and center punch. Drill and countersink basket and foot pivot points the length of their dashed lines using a 1/8" drill bit and a 1/4" to 3/8" countersink.

Step 3 With table flat, cut along dashed lines to separate foot. Drill at points A, B and C using a 1/16" drill bit. Beginning at point A, cut along dashed line (with table flat) to separate inner basket from the outer shape.

Step 4 After measuring the size of the circle or oval basket to be cut out please refer to the chart on page   for the proper bevel. Using the bevel indicated, cut the basket rungs following the solid line. If your table tilts to the left begin your cut at point C and finish at point B. If your table tilts to the right begin your cut at point B and finish at point C. **Note**: It is easier to begin at point C and end at point B.

Step 5 Using the 1/4" roundover bit, rout where indicated on the example below. Sand where needed. Assemble basket and foot with screws at drilled pivot points. Soak in oil according to manufacturer's instructions.

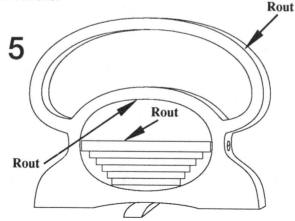

General Basket Instructions (continued)

We have stated a drill bit size and corresponding screw size in the materials listed above. If, however, you choose to use a size other than what is listed, use a drill bit one size smaller than the screws you are using. This will ensure that the screws will fit snugly, providing enough resistance so the basket does not swing freely. You can determine the length of the screw you need for any given pivot point by measuring the length of its dotted line on the pattern. If you wish to counter sink the screw, keep in mind that you will need a shorter length of screw than what the dotted line measured.

Sand any rough edges on the outer shape and the first rung of the basket. If the basket or foot catches on any edges when pivoted, try sanding a little more. For a more refined look use a 1/4" roundover router bit on the edges.

When the basket is completed, soak it in oil according to the manufactures' instructions.

Helpful Hints

Round or Oval baskets - If you have trouble getting the basket to fold out completely (see figure 1a), you may need to adjust your bevel. If you previously used a 6° bevel, try using a 5° or 4°, if you used a 7° bevel, try a 6° or 5°, etc. This will allow the basket to fold out deeper (see figure 1b). If the opposite is happening and the basket rungs are too loose, again you will need to adjust the bevel. If you used a 6° bevel, try a 7° or 8°, if you used a 7° bevel, try an 8° or 9°, etc.

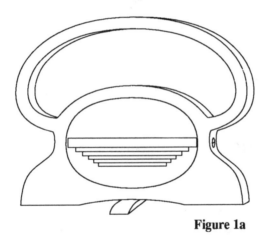
Figure 1a

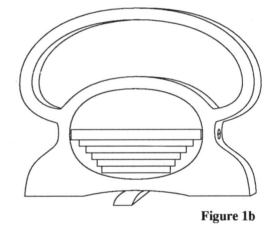
Figure 1b

Round Baskets -
Occasionally the basket will not fold out completely even if the proper bevel was used. Due to the complexity of the grain patterns in some woods, the basket will turn so that the grain does not align after you have cut the basket rungs (see figure 2a). If so, realign the grain by turning the basket rungs clockwise or counter clockwise (see figure 2b), and open the basket.

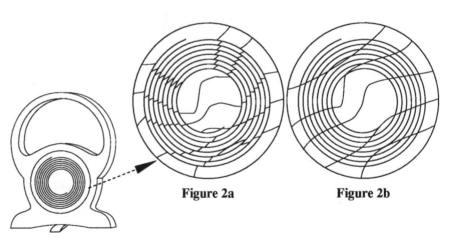
Figure 2a   **Figure 2b**

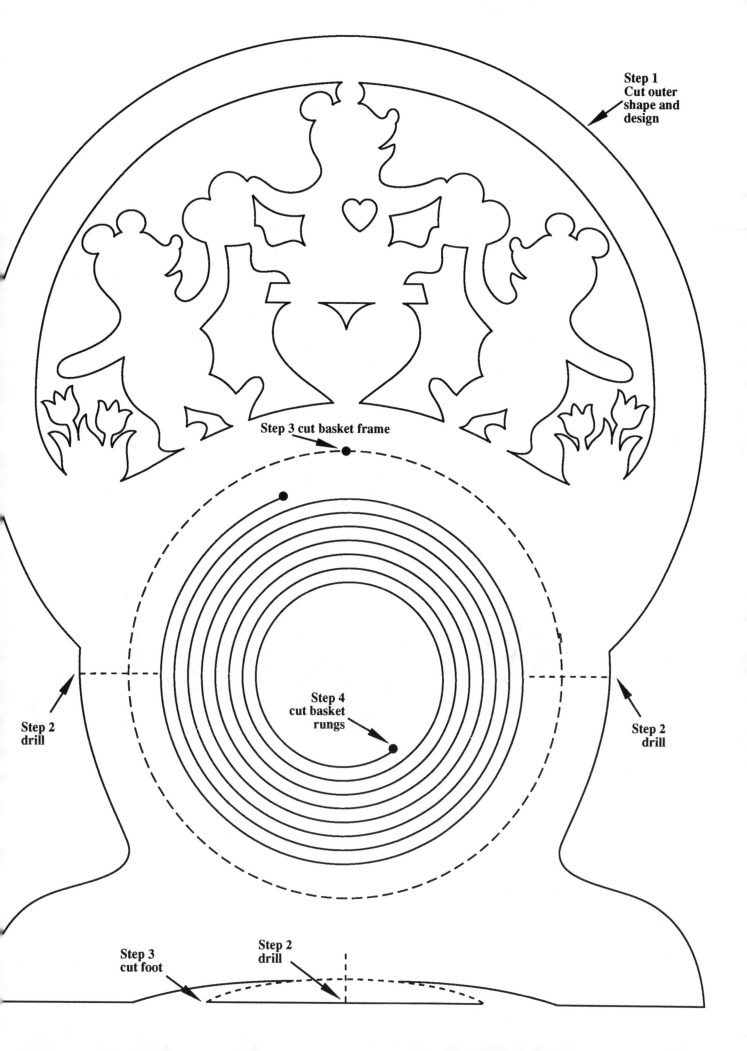

Step 1
Cut outer
shape and
design

Step 3 cut basket frame

Step 2
drill

Step 4
cut basket
rungs

Step 2
drill

Step 3
cut foot

Step 2
drill

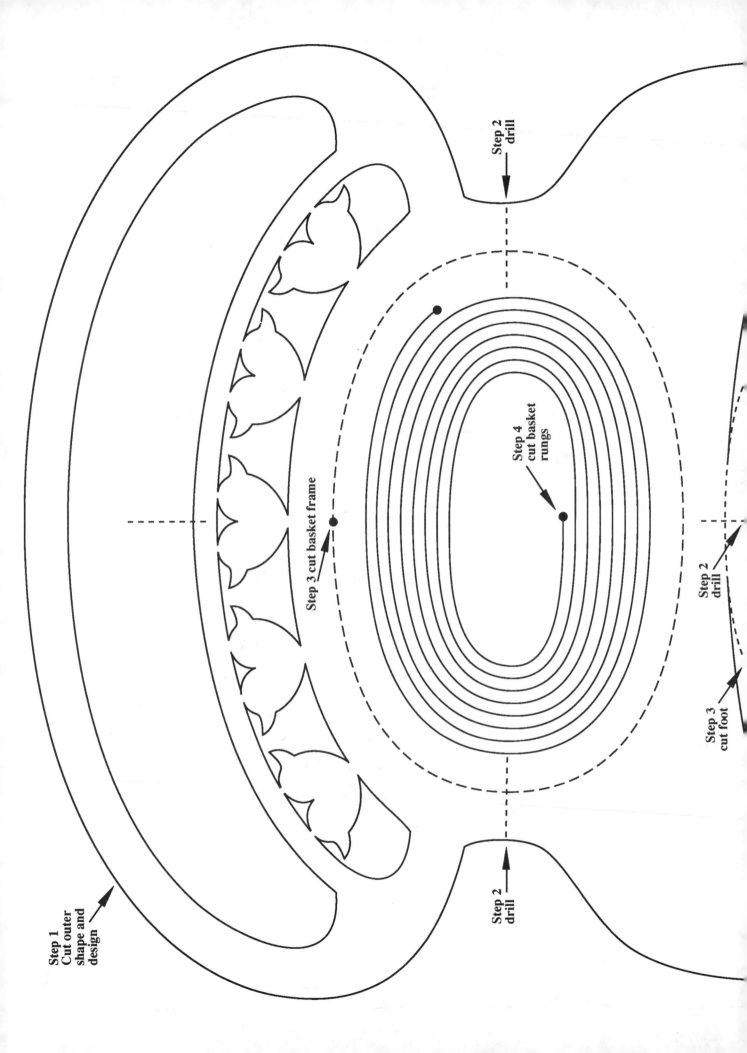

Step 1
Cut outer
shape and
design

Step 3 cut basket frame

Step 2
drill

Step 4
cut basket
rungs

Step 2
drill

Step 2
drill

Step 3
cut foot

Chapter 11

3-Dimensional Scenes

3-DIMENSIONAL SCENES

You can make beautiful 3-dimensional scenes with your scroll saw. (See the color gallery section in the middle of the book to see pieces finished with recommended colors.)

Step by step instructions follow. Note: the squareness of your machine set-up is critical on these projects. Review the chapter on Scroll Saw Basics if necessary before you begin.

General Directions for 3-D Scenes

Although the sizes vary, basically they are all cut the same way with only a few minor exceptions.

Blade used: **#3 double tooth.**

Size of wood: **Specified for each project.**

Table Setting: **Will be at specified angles for each project.**

Wood will be 3/4″ pine and 1/8″ birch door skin or Italian poplar. Size will vary, and will be specified for each project.

Cut the two pieces of wood required for each piece to the exact size by putting one on top of the other and cutting. This is the only way to guarantee they will both be the same. Cut out the oblong pieces on the table saw so that they will be the same size.

Laminate (glue) the thin piece of Italian poplar or birch on the top of the 3/4″ pine, and clamp until dry with spring clamps. **(Photo #41)** After you apply the glue, rub the two surfaces together to spread evenly. This will assure you of a good, tight bond.

Apply the pattern **(photo #42)** and drill the necessary pilot holes (marked by an arrow). These are your starting points when making the inside cuts.

Tilt your table to the degrees specified for each row, and cut out first row. **(Photo #43)** Be sure to cut in the direction of the

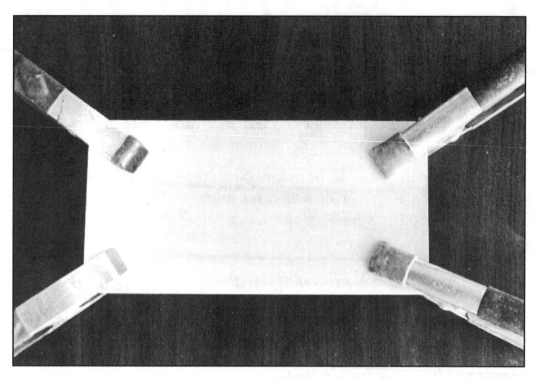

Photo 41 *Laminating thin poplar to pine with spring clamps.*

Photo 42 *Pattern securely affixed, ready to drill pilot holes.*

Photo 43 *Adjusting table angle to make beveled cuts. Example above is tilted 2 1/2 degrees left.*

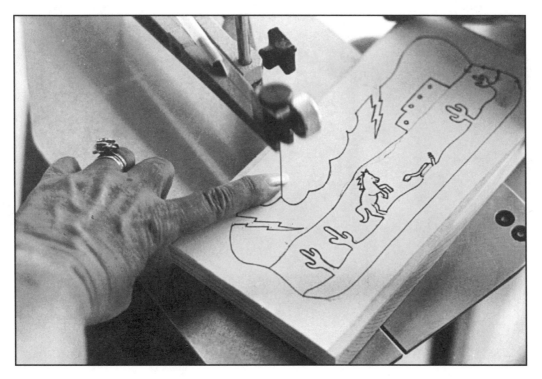

Photo 44 *Blade inserted through pre-drilled pilot hole. Notice finger in position for "pivot point" turn. Make sure you are cutting in direction indicated on patterns.*

arrows, and be sure the angle of the table is correct. Remove each row as it is cut. Remove pattern and set aside. **(See Photo series #44 through 48.)**

After cutting, assemble the piece. Notice that the pieces will only go in one way — either from the back or from the front. This depends on the direction of each cut. **(See photos # 49 through 51.)** This is why it is critical for make the cuts in the direction of the arrows.

Push the pieces in as far as they will go without forcing them. They will lock in that position. When finished these projects are quite intriguing and make quite a conversation piece. **(Photo # 52).**

I have included painting instructions for two of these patterns, but the Southwestern scene is yours to be creative with! Choose your colors wisely, and only paint with a wash of color if you wish to paint- or stain with several different colors of stain. Either way the piece will be beautiful. See specific sizes and special directions for each project at the beginning of each scene.

Photo 45   *Remove outside perimeter after making first cut.*

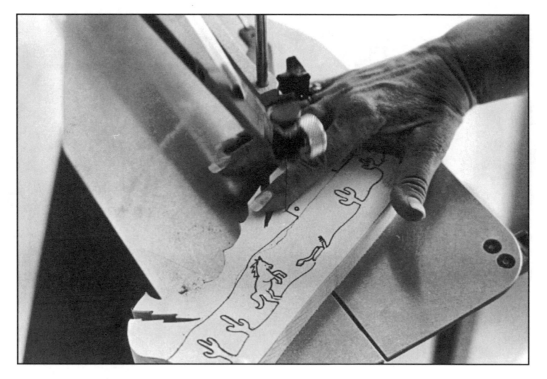

Photo 46   *Cutting out top row. Again, notice finger placed behind blade for accurate cutting on turns and curves.*

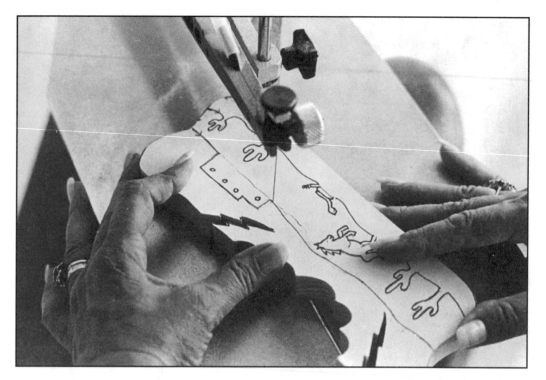

Photo 47   *Smoothly cutting out the second row.*

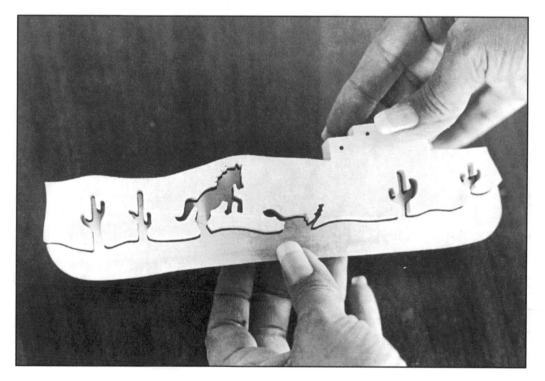

Photo 48   *Third row cut out.*

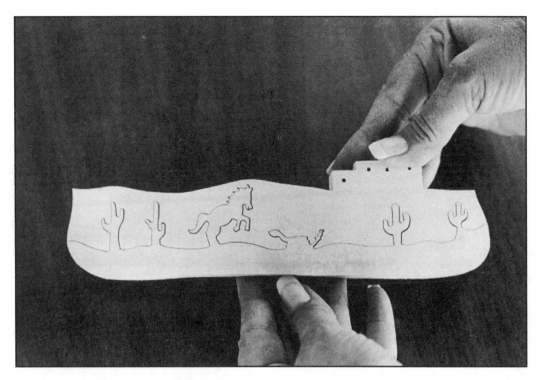

Photo 49   *Setting the second row into the third row from the back.*

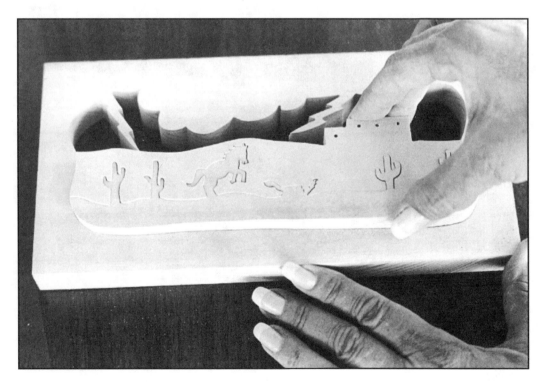

Photo 50   *Set together in frame from top.*

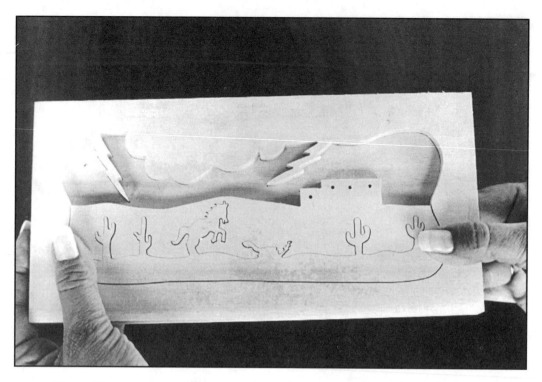

Photo 51   *Push top piece into position from front and push back as far as it will go, locking it into position.*

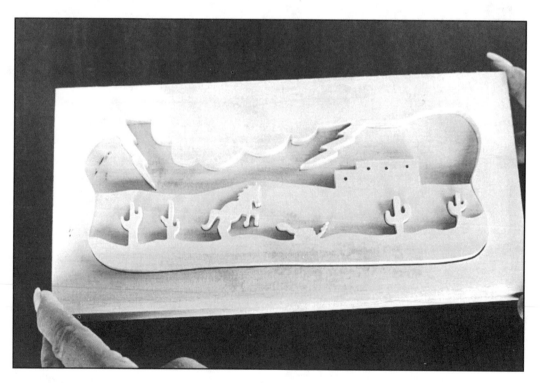

Photo 52   *Finished Southwest scene with rows properly positioned.*

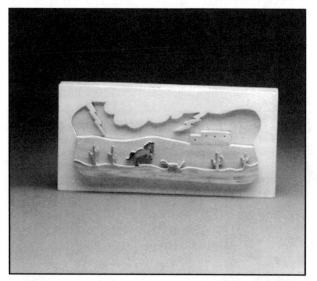

Wood: **10 1/2" x 5 1/2" x 1" pine**
10 1/2" x 5 1/2" x 1/8" Italian poplar,* or birch doorskin*

Blade: **#3 double tooth**

Yellow wood glue, spring clamps, 1/32 drill bit, and hand drill or drill press.

Follow general directions for wood preparation. Drill a hole at the arrow on top of the piece (at lightening bolt). Insert blade through bottom of piece and re-connect the blade into the upper clamp.

Tilt the table 2 degrees to the left. Cut in a clockwise direction (arrow) until you have cut the entire outside perimeter of the scene out. Remove blade, and push the section out through the front of the piece. Set this "frame" aside.

Tilt the table to 3 degrees to the left. Start cutting #2 in a counter-clockwise direction, beginning on the right edge of the piece. Set this section aside when completed.

Tilt the table back to 2 degrees to the left. Start cutting #3 in a counter-clockwise direction (arrow), beginning on the right edge of the wood.

*The Italian poplar can be purchased at your local lumber yard, The birch door skin costs approximately $12.00 for a 4 x 8 foot sheet- poplar about $16.00 for the same size piece. The door skin is more readily available and requires less sanding than the poplar as it is harder wood.

HEART COUNTRY 3-D SCENE

Wood: **11"X 12"X 3/4" pine**
            11"X 12"x 3/4" Italian poplar or
            birch doorskin

Blade: **# 3 double tooth**

Yellow wood glue, spring clamps, 1/32" drill bit, and a hand drill or drill press.

Consult general directions for 3-D scenes as above.

Glue the pine and thin wood together. Due to the shape of this piece, you won't be able to use the table saw, so cut out the entire heart shape with your scroll saw. You will also need to cut out the stand from pine using the scroll saw.

Drill a pilot hole at the left side of the heart at the arrow. Insert blade from bottom and re-connect the blade into the upper clamp.

Sail Fish 3-D Scene
enlarge 25%

CUT OUTSIDE PERIMITER 1st Then tilt Table 2° L -- do 2nd cut. Tilt Table 2½° L
do 3rd cut ... Tilt Table 3° L, do Final Cut.

CUT OUTSIDE PERIMETER FIRST

COUNTER CLOCKWISE 4

COUNTER CLOCKWISE 3

CLOCKWISE CUTTING

START here 2nd

Tilt the table 2 degrees to the left. Cut in a clockwise direction (arrow) until you have cut the entire outside perimeter of the scene out. Remove blade, and push the section out through the front of the piece. Set this "frame" aside.

Tilt the table to 3 degrees to the left. Start cutting #2 in a counter-clockwise direction, beginning on the right edge of the piece. Set this section aside when completed.

Tilt the table back to 2 degrees to the left.

Sand and seal with Delta clear wood sealer. Allow to dry and lightly sand again. Tack.

Painting Directions:

Palette: Delta Ceramcoat	
Midnight	*Black*
White	*Black Green*
Autumn Brown	*Burnt Sienna*
Blue Wisp	*Leprechaun*

Brushes: **3/4" flat   #5 round   1/2" angle
10/0 liner or an extra fine
Black Sharpie permanent marker.**

Other supplies: Delta's clear wood sealer, and clear satin varnish.

Remove the center section. Begin by painting only the "frame." Using a 3/4" flat brush, dampen it and "paint" the entire section with water. You don't want a flood of water here — just enough to penetrate the wood. This will give you a good base for your base coat, without much streaking. Now quickly wash the entire area with Autumn Brown, until you have a very light stain on the wood. Set aside to dry.

Transfer pattern to center piece.

Use the largest brush possible for base coating. If you feel the need to go to a smaller brush, use the #5 round for the trees and houses.

Pick up the top piece of the inside section and base the sky in Midnight.

Base the snow on the other sections in White. Finish the wooden base in White as well.

Base the cabin in Autumn Brown. Cabin roof is Burnt Sienna. Shade the roof of the cabin with a light float of Black and float the left side and the top of the door and windows in black.

Base the church in Blue Wisp. The roof is Burnt Sienna. Float the details on the church with a mix of Blue Wisp and Black. (Mix in just enough Black to darken the Blue Wisp.)

Base all the trees in Black Green.

Top row of trees: Load the angle brush with Black Green. Then add White to the longest tip of the brush. Pounce just the knife edge of the brush up and down to form the branches of pine needles on the trees. This gives it the effect of snow on the tips of the branches. Always start at the bottom branches and work your way to the top. Make each layer of branches a little smaller so the tree comes to a point at the top.

Bottom layer of trees: Load the angle brush with Leprechaun, the tip with White again, and finish as you did on the top row of trees.

Shade the hills behind the house with White + Black (just enough to darken slightly). Shade under all of the trees with Leprechaun.

Paint stars with 10/0 liner and very thin White. See diagram below.

Paint the base in the same way as the snow and trees in the upper section of the piece.

Transfer writing when dry, and apply with Sharpie marker.

This piece can be left as is, or apply a final coat of Clear Satin Varnish.

SAIL FISH 3-D SCENE

This is a rather attractive piece, and looks good even when left unpainted. There are three different types of material that work well for this project:

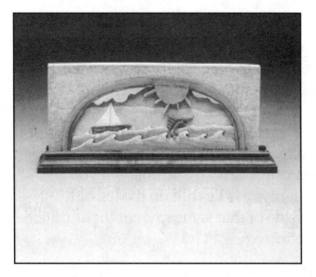

#1. Corian Tile

#2. Pine

#3. Red Oak

Size of project: **13"x 5¼"x 3/4"**

Blades:

    If you cut from Corian Tile use a #2 Ultra blade

    If you cut from pine use a #3 double tooth

    If you cut from oak use a #7 double tooth or a #2 Ultra

Angle of table:

> **1st row:** Table should be square to cut the outside perimeter.
>
> **2nd row:** 2 degrees left. Cut clockwise (left to right).
>
> **3rd row:** 3 degrees left. Cut counter clockwise (right to left)
>
> **4th row:** 2 degrees left Cut counter clockwise.

1st row: Cut out the outside perimeter.

2nd row: Be sure to watch the pivot points around the sun rays. Due to the angle of the table, some of these turns will be very difficult to do. If you over-cut or under-cut a line – DO NOT BACK UP! Compensate for it on the other side when you get to it. If you back up your mistake will show ten times worse than if you just compensate. Remember, once you remove the pattern the mistakes won't show. As an example – if you accidentally cut one of the sun rays a little thin on the left side, when you get to the right side of that same ray, cut to the outside to thicken it. Simple but effective, isn't it?

3rd Row: Cutting from right to left, cut the wave, go around the tail of the fish on the bottom and up to meet the other half of the wave. Continue across the wave until you have completed this row.

Remove this row, remove pattern section and set aside.

4th Row: Cutting from right to left again, cut the wave, go around the bottom of the fish until the wave section is free. Remove that small section of the wave, and start cutting the rest of the sailfish beginning at the right side of him (her)? Work your way up and around the sword, sail and down his back until he is free. Take him out. Continue to cut across the waves to the boat. Do no separate the boat from the waves under it (that is just a painting line) but cut up the bow, over the top of the sails, down the middle of the sails, and so forth until you have the piece completely cut out.

Put all the sections back in one by one starting with the top section. Remember, the sections will only go in from one direction. The "sky" can only be put in from the front, and the two bottom sections can only be put in from the back. Push them as far as you can to lock them in position. Now flatten them out and sand smooth. Separate them and seal each section with Delta's Clear wood sealer. DO NOT SEAL THE CUT EDGES ON THE CENTER SECTION! This will cause the pieces to swell, and they will not go back in. If you have chosen to work on Corian, sealing is not necessary.

If you choose to paint, the directions follow. (Yes, you can paint on the Corian.)

Painting Directions

Palette: Delta Ceramcoat	
Rain Forest	**Ice Storm**
Blue Wisp	**White**
Dolphin	**Crocus**
Manganese Blue	**Wisteria**
Cardinal Red	**Black**
Silver	

Brushes: #12 flat   #5 Round

Additional supplies: Delta Clear satin varnish.

Water: Base in Rain Forest. Float top of waves in Blue Wisp, highlight with White at tips.

Lower Sky area: Base in Ice storm. Float cloud streaks in Dolphin. Float again in Blue Wisp and highlight in White.

Upper Sky area: Base in Ice Storm, and wash over with Crocus. Float Blue Wisp around skyline. Continue on both sides of sun. Dry brush some very faint Blue Wisp in sky.

Float sun in Crocus + Cardinal Red. Highlight with Crocus on left side only.

Sail Fish: Base in Silver. Float Manganese Blue across back, up sword and mouth, and inside stripes on his sail. With Manganese Blue + a small amount of Black float on opposite sides of stripes on his "sail". Reverse float Wisteria down center of body and on "sail".

Boat: Wash in Manganese Blue. (keep it light) Float Manganese Blue + Black across bow of boat, and down side. Base Sails white. Float with wash of Crocus.

Dab a little more white on the tips of the waves if you think they need it.

Allow to dry. Sand lightly with a crumpled brown paper bag. Tack, and apply a coat of Delta's Satin Varnish to each separate piece. DO NOT VARNISH WITH PIECES TOGETHER – they will stick!

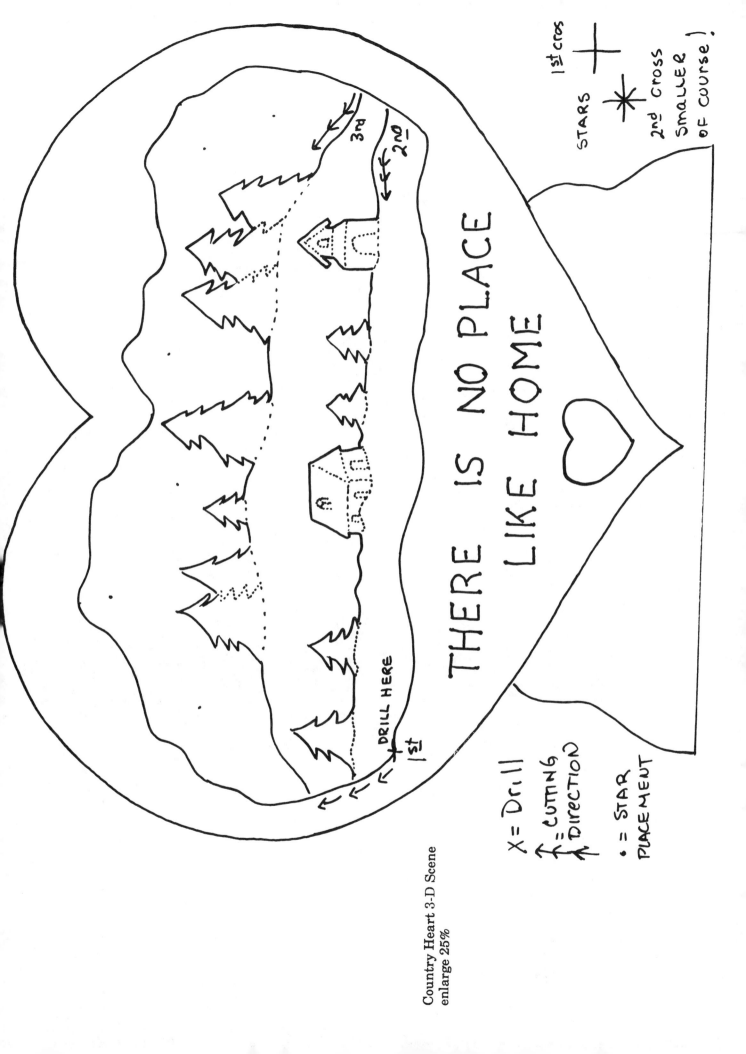

THERE IS NO PLACE
LIKE HOME

Country Heart 3-D Scene
enlarge 25%

X = Drill

↑ CUTTING
↑ DIRECTION

• = STAR
PLACEMENT

DRILL HERE

1st

2nd

3rd

1st cros

STARS

2nd Cross
SMALLER
OF COURSE!

Chapter 12

Alphabets and Things

ALPHABETS AND THINGS

I have included a few alphabets for you to do something terribly clever with. If you wish to do a lot of letter work I recommend you purchase permanent templates. See companies listed on source page.

The Apple Alphabet puzzle here is a "tray" puzzle. Please read the general directions for tray puzzles before you begin.

Apple Alphabet Puzzle
Wood: **11" x 14" x 3/4" pine (top piece)**
11" x 14" x 1/8" Birch door skin or plywood (bottom piece)

Blade: **#7 double tooth and # 5 double tooth.**

Directions: Spray glue the pattern to the pine piece. Install the #7 blade.

Cut both pieces of wood at the same time by stacking them together and securing them with masking tape.

Remove masking tape and set the thin piece aside. Router the top of the 1" pine with a 1/4" roundover. Drill a hole in an inconspicuous spot for every letter, and in the inside of every letter that requires an inside cut. (the A,B,D,O,P,Q, & R,) Install your # 5 blade . Undo the top of your blade, insert it through the bottom of your wood, re-attach in the upper blade clamp, tension, and cut. You will repeat this step for each letter . Cut the centers of the letters first, and then cut the actual shape of the letters out.

Warning: If you do not cut square into the wood, or if you push off to one side it may cause the letters to fit improperly. Concentrate when doing this.

Remove each letter as you cut, so it does not jam in the blade hole in your machine. (This also gives you a good opportunity to check your cut!)

When you have finished cutting the entire alphabet out, sand all of the pieces, and set aside while you glue the top and the bottom together. Do this very carefully as you do not want any excess glue to dry in the holes. Put a thin line of glue about 1/2″ inside the apple, lay the pine piece on top and move back and forth gently to spread the glue. Check to see if any glue has oozed out, and wipe it off with a damp cloth. Line up the two pieces, and clamp.

Check the inside of the holes for glue, and remove any at this time with a very wet Q-Tip.

After the apple has dried, I like to sand the edge with my 1″ belt sander to remove any glue that may have sneaked up on me, or to even the front and back
in the event there was slippage when the clamps were applied.

You may put the alphabet back in when the piece is completely dry.

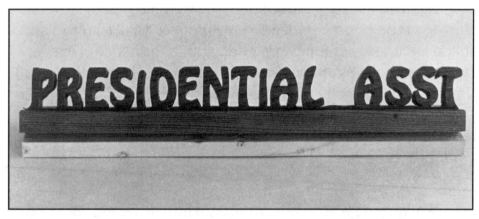

Lettering projects make great gifts and are popular craft show items.
Nameplates are fun and easy to make.

Painting Instructions for Apple Alphabet

Sand, tack to remove sawdust, and seal the wood pieces Then lightly sand again.

Brushes needed: #12 flat 1″ sponge brush #1 liner and a stylus.

Palette: Delta Ceramcoat.
Crimson
Forest Green
White
Brown Iron Oxide

Remove all of the letters, and with the sponge brush basecoat the apple in Crimson. Switch to the #12 brush and base the leaves in Forest Green, and the stem in Brown Iron Oxide. Since this is a child's toy, I am keeping the painting very simple, with no shading.

Base coat the letters in White.

With the liner, paint Crimson comma strokes. With the stylus make little country hearts (two dots side by side, and with the smallest end of the stylus pull out the heart tail).

I chose not to put any finish at all on this, but left it "country" finished. If you prefer a little shinier finish, use Deltas' satin varnish.

When dry, put the alphabets in their appropriate places, and watch the smiles.

On the following pages, I have included some extra alphabets for you to do what ever you want with, so there will be no specific directions or projects for them. On the source page you will find two excellent sources for lettering guides. Using a letter guide rather than tracing makes the work neater, and it goes much faster. There are many types available. My favorite are

---

the very small guides for making key chains that require no inside cuts. These go over very well at craft shows, and take very little time to cut. Call or write the companies listed in the back for a catalog.

ABCDEFGHIJK
LMNOPQRSTUV
WXYZ&abcdefgh
ijklmnopqrstuvw
xyz1234567890

ABCDEFG
HIJKLMNO
PQRSTUVW
XYZ&abcde
fghijklmno
pqrstuvwx
yz12345
67890

ABCDEF
GHIJKLM
NOPQRST
UVWXYZ
&abcdefghijk
lmnopqrstuv
wxyz1234
567890

ABCDEFGHIJ
KLMNOPQRST
UVWXYZ&abc
defghijklmnop
qrstuvwxyz
1234567890

ABCDEFGH
IJKLMNOPQ
RSTUVWXY
Z&abcdefghij
klmnopqrstuv
wxyz
1234567890

ABCDEFGHI
JKLMNOPQR
STUVWXYZ
&abcdefghijk
lmnopqrstu
vwxyz
1234567890

ABCDEFGHI
JKLMNOPQ
RSTUVWX
YZ&abcde
fghijklmno
pqrstuvwx
yz1234
567890

ABCDEFG
HIJKLMNO
PQRSTUV
WXYZ&ab
cdefghijk
lmnopqrst
uvwxyz12
34567890

ABCDEFG
HIJKLMNO
PQRSTUVW
XYZ&abcde
fghijklmnop
qrstuvwxyz
1234567890

ABCDEFGHI
JKLMNOPQ
RSTUVWXYZ
&abcdefgh
ijklmnopqr
stuvwxyz
1234567890

Chapter 13

Christmas Projects

CHRISTMAS PROJECTS

SNOWFLAKE ORNAMENTS

As you will notice, some of these are the same patterns as the trivet and coaster sets. I have printed smaller versions for you to make some beautiful Fretwork Christmas ornaments.

General directions

Wood for all snowflakes will be 1/8″ double faced "Baltic birch" (Good both sides).

Luan Ply is thin plywood that is smooth on one side only. This is the wood they make doors out of - commonly called "doorskin". You can find the Luan at most lumber supply stores. It is much less expensive, and can be used in place of Baltic birch when both sides of a project will not be visible.

You will be using a # 5 double tooth blades for all snowflakes. All snowflakes (with the exception of the oak snowflake) can be "stack cut" at least 6 deep. Advanced woodcrafters may even be able to cut more out at a time. Beware of the fact that as you stack cut higher, you will encounter some difficulty in maintaining a perpendicular cut.

Cut the wood to proper size for pattern.

Stack number of desired pieces together and apply masking tape around the outside edge to secure.

Apply pattern with spray glue. Drill 1/8″ hole where indicated for hanging.

Drill pilot holes for all inside cuts.

Do all inside cuts first, removing each piece as you cut it.

Cut along outside perimeter. Remove masking tape when finished.

Sand if necessary. Seal with Delta clear wood sealer.

Painting Directions :

Paint all surfaces with Delta Ceramcoat White.

When dry seal with Deltas Jewelry Glaze While still wet sprinkle "Glitter" on them. Do not cover heavily with glitter or they will look cheap. Use just enough to make them sparkle in the lights.

After drying, string a gold metallic cord through the hole and hang.

These ornaments can be the start of a wonderful family holiday tradition. Make this a project for the whole family - let them decorate the snowflakes as fancy as they want. Have each person sign the back with the date and their name.

PAINTED SNOWFLAKE ORNAMENT

See color section for completed project in full color.

Wood: **1 pc. 7" x 7" 1/4" Oak**

Blade: **#5 reverse tooth**

Supplies: **8" of 1/8" red, green or gold ribbon**
1/8" drill bit

Cut wood to proper size, Apply pattern and cut. (there are no inside cuts on this snowflake)

Drill a 1/8" hole where indicated to hang ornament on tree.

Sand if necessary. Seal with Delta clear wood sealer.

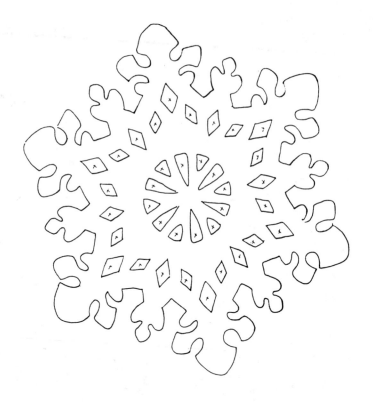

Painting Directions:

Palette: *Delta Ceramcoat*

Dark Night	**Brown Iron Oxide**
Forest Green	**Cactus**
Seminole	**Black**
Dark Forest	**White**
Lime	**Golden Brown**

Brushes needed: #12 flat   #6 flat   #5 round
10/0 liner

Finish: **Delta Jewelry glaze**

Trace pattern. Apply pattern to wood piece with graphite.

With the # 12 flat brush, wash the entire outer area and edges in Golden Brown. You want the grain of the wood to show through. Therefore, thin the paint in a 1-3 ratio (one part paint to three parts water.)

Base Coating:
Sky: **Midnight   Road and House: Autumn Brown.
Hedge: Forest Green**

Back Hill: Cactus   Front Hill: Seminole.

Shading and detail: Base coating should always be done with the larger brush. If you find this too difficult use to a round brush instead.

Back hill: Float on top with BIO

Front Hill: Float with Dark Forest

Cabin: Float BIO under roof, on windows & doors, on left side of roof, and float "boards" on cabin.

Float behind hedge, behind front hill, and pot holes in road, with Blk .

Highlight top of front hill with White, and "Mop " to blend.

Dry brush some BIO & DF highlights on hills.

Trees: BIO the bases of each tree. Load the # 6 flat brush with DF. Now pick up some Lime on the corner of the brush. Hold the brush straight up and down - pounce lightly up and down, keeping the lighter color to the outside of the limbs. Start at the bottom of the tree and work your way up . Do not overlap the branches, but keep them light and airy. Highlight with white at outer branches and at the very top of the tree to resemble a light snow.

Note: If you prefer you can paint the branches of the tree with your liner. Dip liner brush in DF and then in Lime. Paint each branch separately and keep them airy.

Sheep: Dip a Q-tip in white and pat on for the bodies and heads. With Blk and the round brush add the feet and ears.

Float under the sheep and trees with DF.

Highlight the doors and windows in the cabin with crocus.

Fence: With your liner and white, paint the fence and the rails. With liner and thin black,paint very delicate lines on the left and across the top of the posts.

Shade under fence with a float of DF.

Stipple hedge with Cactus, Seminole, and finally Straw at the top of the hedge.

With your liner and very thin white paint, make stars. Make a cross first, then do another much smaller cross in the center of the first one (see diagram on pattern). Add a little dot of Jewelry glaze. While wet sprinkle with "Diamond Dust" or glitter. When all is dry, finish the entire piece with two coats of Jewelry glaze. Add ribbon and hang.

GINGERBREAD MAN CANDLE HOLDERS

Wood: **Pine - two pieces**

Supplies: **1″ Forstner bit**
1/2″ Roundover bit.
2-1″x 6″ white candle.
Spray glue & Graphite paper

Blade: **# 9 double tooth or #5 Ultra**

Table: **Must be square!**

Special instruction: Be sure to tension your saw 1/4 to 1/2 turn more than what is considered normal by the manufacturer, and feed square into the blade.

Apply pattern with spray glue, and cut the Gingerbread man out. If you are real clever, you can trace the little hearts onto a piece of 1/8" birch ply and cut them out separately. Stack them to cut. If you don't feel terribly clever today, you can paint them on. They look cute both ways.

You will need to drill a 1″ hole in the center of the top of his head for a candle. Use the Forstner bit for this. I recommend clamping the piece onto your drill press if you have one. Drill the hole 1″ deep, for the candle to set well into the hole.

Put a 1/2″ Roundover all the way around except at the bottom of the feet. Leave this part flat so they will stand firmly. Roundover both sides.

Suggestion:
These make a cute table arrangement if you put them in groups of three, with a little Christmas foliage around their feet, as well as a ribbon around the bottom of the Candle. I have included 3 different sizes for you to choose from. The specifications above are for the largest one.

I first made these over 15 years ago and we are still using these every holiday season.

Painting Instructions

Brushes needed: **1" Flat and #10/0 liner**

Supplies: **Deltas clear wood sealer and Clear Satin Varnish.**

Palette: Delta Ceramcoat.

Maple Sugar	**Golden Brown**
Black	**Coral**
White	**Tomato Spice**

Sand, tack to remove lint and dust. Seal. While this is drying, trace the pattern. When dry, line the pattern up with wood piece and hold in place while you insert the graphite paper underneath. Trace over the lines with a stylus or red pen. (You will be able to see where you have traced if using a red pen.)

With your 1" brush and the Maple Sugar, base in the entire Gingerbread Man.

Do the sides and the back, but do not paint inside the hole. You want to cover him well, so if need be, give him another coat after the first is dry.

With the same brush, float Golden Brown all the way around the edge. You want him to look slightly browned at the edges like a real cookie. (At least they look that way in my oven.) Float both sides.

On the front side you will be doing the "icing" decorations.

Take a puddle of white paint, and mix 1 part water to two parts paint. With your liner, and white paints, do the little rounded zig-zag decoration. These zig-zags are ont applied on the back side.

With Black on your liner paint his eyes, eyebrows, mouth line, and his nose.

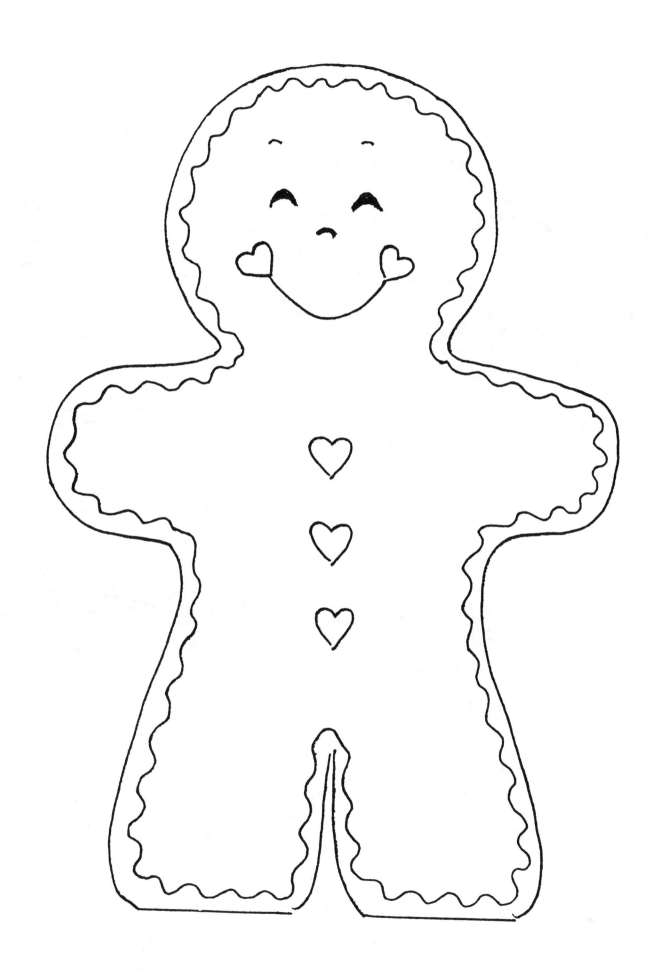

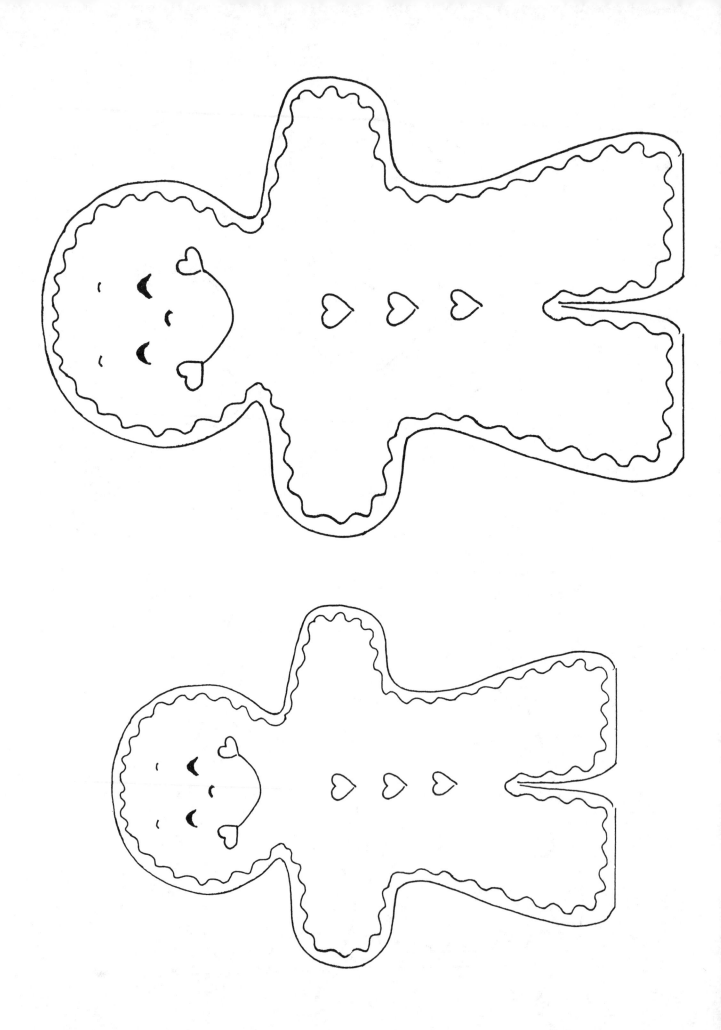

The hearts are painted with Tomato Spice, floated with Candy Bar on the left side. If you haven't perfected the floating technique yet, just skip this part.

If you were brave enough to cut the little hearts out of the ply, paint them the same way, and glue in place with yellow wood glue.

When it is dry, finish with one or two coats of Clear Satin Varnish.

Legend has it that after something has been painted and you leave it for a while, when you return the "Tole painting Fairy" will have already been there to fix any little mistakes.

SANTA DOOR GREETING

Wood: **12" x 15" x 1/2" pine or plywood**

Supplies: **6 1/2" hole buttons (plugs) — slightly rounded on top**
Yellow wood glue
Graphite paper and spray glue

Blade: **# 5 Reverse tooth blade**

Spray the paper pattern, and apply to the wood piece.

Drill holes for blade insertion where indicated by X's.

Make all inside cuts and remove cut out sections. Finish cutting the rest of the piece out. Be sure to keep the sharp points on the Holly leaves.

Sand the piece with a hand sander if you have one. Use a tack cloth to remove any residue before proceeding with the painting directions.

I designed this piece for those of you who have never painted but have always wanted to try. In fact I am making it a "paint by number" type.

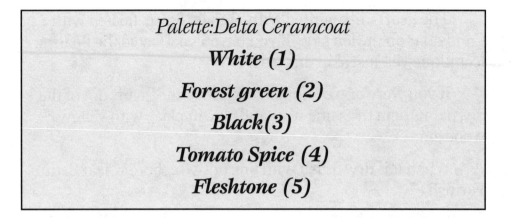

Palette:Delta Ceramcoat
White (1)
Forest green (2)
Black(3)
Tomato Spice (4)
Fleshtone (5)

Brushes needed: **# 12 Flat   #5 round   # 10/0 liner 2" foam brush**

Other supplies: A plastic lid to put the paint colors on. A Palette to blend the paint on. Delta clear wood sealer, Deltas clear satin varnish, paper towels and Q-tips.

Pour a little sealer in a small container (paper cups are fine). Dip the foam brush in it and let it absorb the sealer. Put a paper towel down to catch the drips, and apply sealer to every inch of the piece — edges, front, back, etc. Allow to dry, and sand if needed. Use a tack cloth to remove any dust and residue.

Wet the foam brush and squeeze the water out. Paint the leaves with Forest Green.

Wet the #12 Flat, touch just the edge of it to the paper towel to get rid of the excess water, and dip it into a little puddle of the Fleshtone. Paint Santa's face. Don't worry about getting the paint elsewhere as it will be covered. Do not apply paint too thick. You want a nice even coat without leaving ridges where the paint meets the unpainted areas.

If you are getting streaks in your finish, you are probably using too much water.

When you "load" your brushes with paint, don't forget to work the paint into the brush a little by laying the bristles of the brush down to the left, and then to the right, as you sweep back and forth. Do this just a couple of times to blend the paint into the brush - don't take a big glob of paint to the wood piece. This will give you a smoother first coat!

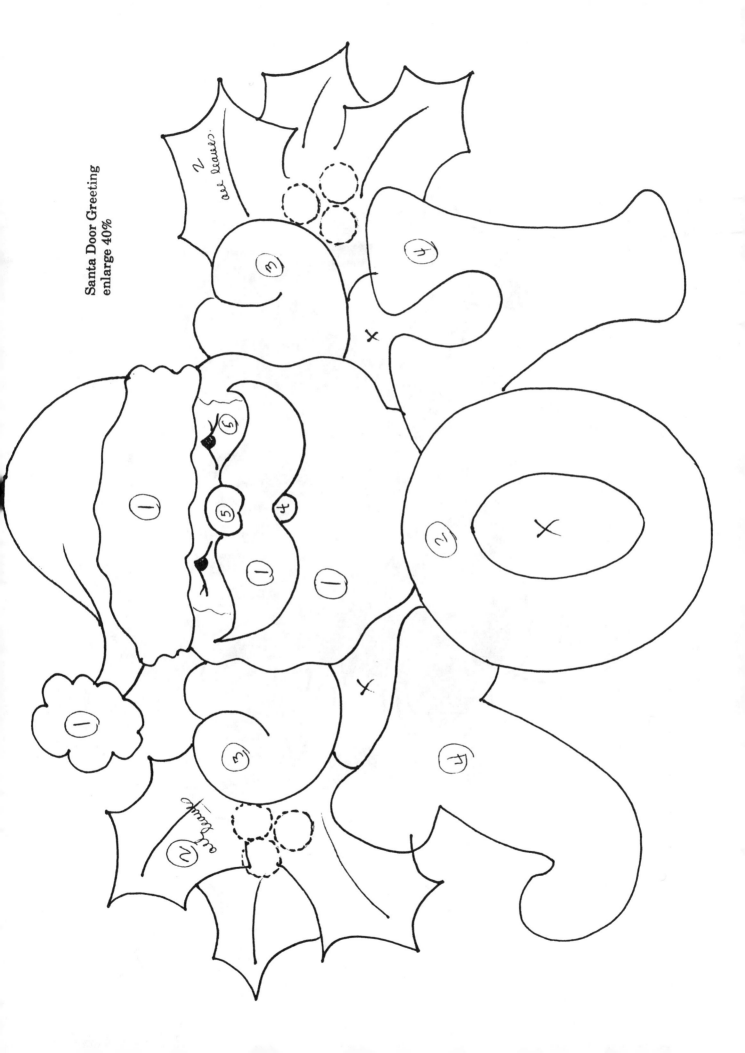

Santa Door Greeting
enlarge 40%

Merry Christmas Wallhanging
enlarge 33%

With the same brush and the same method, paint all the areas indicated with the proper colors. With the round brush, and some Tomato Spice, fill in his mouth.

With the liner and Black paint that has been thinned with water (1 - 3 ratio), paint eyes, mustache line, veins on the leaves, as well as the lines that separate the leaves. Paint the little fold line on hat as well.

Mix a tiny bit of white with the black and paint the crease in his mittens. Paint the buttons Tomato Spice, and when dry glue in the circles where indicated.

For those of you who are more advanced painters, you will want to go ahead and float in all the proper places, with a darker shade of the color used in the section you are floating. Mix the palette colors necessary to achieve the darker tones.

Sand lightly with a brown paper bag that you have crumpled to soften. Remove any loose residue, and finish with two coats of clear satin varnish.

MERRY CHRISTMAS WALL HANGING

Wood: **15" x 9" x 1" pine**

Blade: **#5**

Table: **Square**

Drill Bit: **1/6"**

Make a copy of the pattern.

Cut the pine to size above and spray glue to wood surface.

Drill pilot holes in all blacked out areas in preparation for making the inside cuts. (Do not drill into the holly berries.)

Make inside cuts and remove scrap before cutting out along perimeter.

After all cuts are completed, sand with 200 grit sand paper. Tack to remove any residue. Seal wood with clear wood sealer before painting.

Painting Directions:

> *Palette: Delta Ceramcoat*
>
> **Tomato Spice**
>
> **Forest Green**
>
> **Black**
>
> **White**
>
> **Metallic Gold (optional)**

Brushes: 1" flat   #10 flat   #5 round   10/0 liner

Crumple up a 6" piece of brown bag. Uncrumple and use this to sand off any rough edges the sealer may have left. Do this carefully as this project requires a very smooth painting surface Wipe with a smooth cloth to remove any residue before continuing.

Trace pattern and apply to the wood with graphite paper.

With the 1" brush and Forest Green, base coat the leaves. Use smaller brushes as necessary for smaller areas. Use very little water with the paint. You want a dense coat of paint.

With the #10 flat and Tomato Spice, base in the lettering. Do not paint the berries at this time. Allow project to dry until the wood is no longer cool to the touch, then sand again with the paper bag.

Shade (float) the leaves with a paint mixture of two parts Forest Green to one part White, using the #10 brush. Float the top of each leaf and the top of the center vein.

Mix two parts Forest Green with one part Black. Float this mixture under each leaf where it touches another leaf. Float down on the opposite side of the vein where you floated the FG/W color above.

Outline the lettering with a 10/0 liner and a thinned Black paint — two parts water to one part paint.

Paint a broken line down the middle of the lettering with thinned White or the Metallic Gold. Use the same color to pull some little squiggly lines out form under the berries — which get painted last.

Finally, berries are painted in Tomato Spice. Use a brush handle that is approximately 1/4″ inch thick. Dip the handle into s puddle of Tomato Spice. Keep the handle straight up and use this to dot each berry. Redip the handle for each berry. After the berries have dried, you may wish to paint a small comma stroke on the right side of each berry as a highlight.

Due to the thickness of the paint on the berries, allow this to dry for a minimum of one hour. When dry use the brown paper bag to smooth out the surface. Wipe one last time to remove any residue.

Apply a coat of clear varnish. Hang with a small saw-tooth hanger.

Don't forget to sign your work!

SANTA WREATH

See color ssection for full color photograph of the completed project.

Cutting Directions:

Wood: **1 piece 10 x 10 x 1″ Pine**
                  1 piece 3″ x 12″ x 1/4″ Pine

Blade: **#3 double tooth scroll saw blade or a #5 reverse tooth.**

                  Spray adhesive
                  5 feet of 1/8" satin ribbon. (color of your choice.) Rattail cord, ribbon, or gold chain
                  1/8"&1/4" wood drill bits
                  1/4" roundover bit

Cut wood to size

Apply the heart pattern to the 1″ pine piece with spray glue. Be sure to spray only the paper

pattern, not the wood itself. Cut out. Apply pattern for the small pieces to the 1/4″ pine piece, and cut out.

Round over the edges of the heart with the router. Round both sides.

Drill a 1/4″ hole where indicated on Santa's hands, and on the wreath.

Drill 1/8″ holes in the small pieces to hang them by.

Sand and seal all of the pieces.

DO NOT ASSEMBLE UNTIL AFTER PAINTING IS COMPLETED.

Painting Instructions

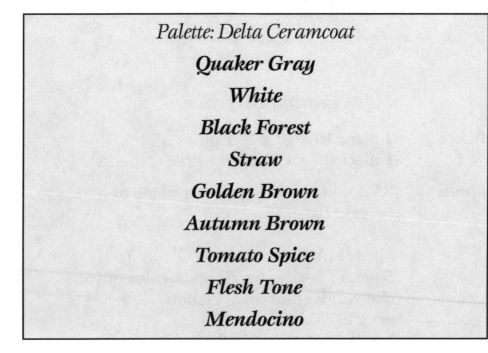

Palette: Delta Ceramcoat

Quaker Gray

White

Black Forest

Straw

Golden Brown

Autumn Brown

Tomato Spice

Flesh Tone

Mendocino

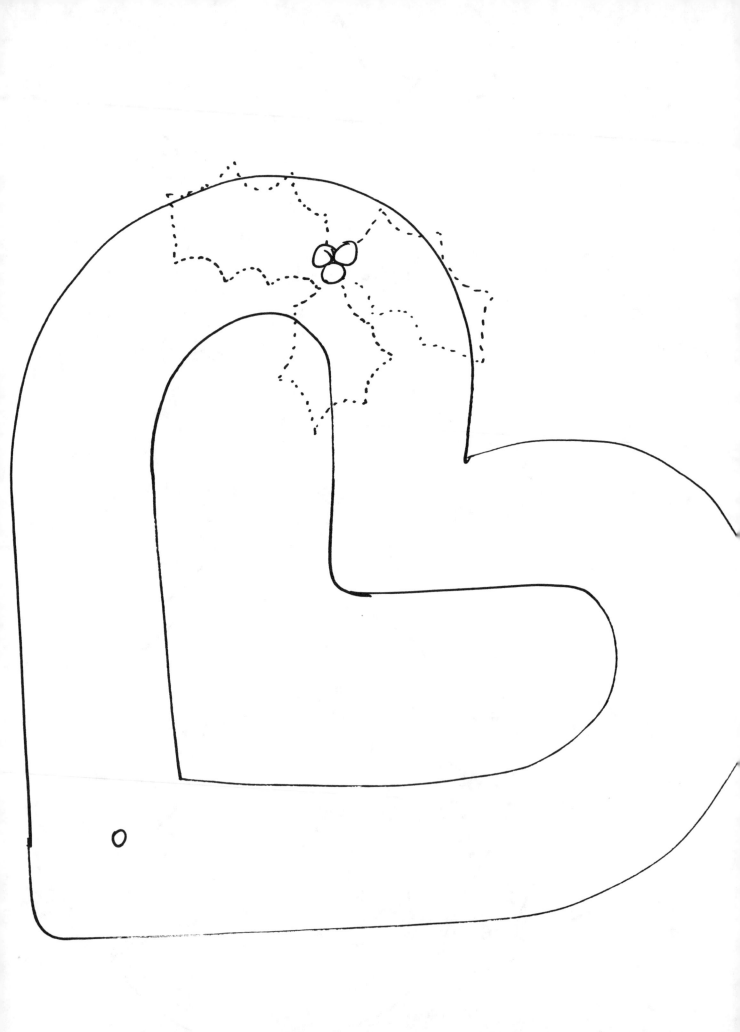

Brushes: 1" foam brush   #12 flat   #5 round   10/0 liner

Supplies: J.W. White lightning   gauzeneutral color paste wax.

Instructions:

Sand, and seal with WL. When dry, lightly sand again and tack.

White: Base coat entire Santa and candy cane.
   Set aside to dry.

Dark Forest: With sponge brush or 1" brush, base the wreath, the small Christmas tree, and the holly.

Autumn Brown: Base coat teddy bear ,trunk of tree.

Golden Brown: Base coat gingerbread man.

Apply pattern to Santa, dolly, and candy cane. The small pieces are better off freehanded due to their size. Trace pattern on if necessary.

Black: Base Santa's mittens ,dolly's shoes.

Fleshtone: Base Santa's face, dolly's face, hands and leg areas. Do not worry about overlapping onto the unpainted areas at this time. You will be covering this over later.

Tomato Spice: Base in Santa's suit, hat and the little heart. Put stripes on candy cane.

Straw: Base in star and dolly's hair.

Quaker Gray: Base in Santa's beard, mustache .

White: Eyebrows on Santa, and dolly's dress.

Shading:

Dark Forest and Black:

Float around outside edge of wreath, small tree, and one side of the holly leaves.

Fleshtone and Tomato Spice:

Float Santa's cheeks, and under his hat, the edges of his face, and behind his mustache. Shade little girl's face and add cheeks.

White:

Highlight Santa's cheeks and over his nose. Highlight behind his eyes. Do a back to back float on the candy cane to highlight. Float a section of Santa's glove to highlight.

Mendocino:

Shade around hat and sleeves, under beard and cuffs, and on the little heart. Float dollies dress to bring our the sleeves etc. Paint Santa's mouth.

Autumn Brown:

Float gingerbread man and one side of each point on the star.

Dark Forest and White:

Float the holly veins, and the opposite side of each leave that you floated earlier.

Autumn Brown and Black:

Float the teddy bears joints, and under his chin as well as around the outside edges.

Detail Work:

Santa's eyes are blue with black pupils. Paint the entire eye blue. Dot the pupil black with a stylus. Dollies eyes are dotted black with stylus. Both have a small white highlight. With your liner do the shape of Santa's eye. Paint the teddy's' nose and mouth. Dot his eyes with the stylus.

Gingerbread Man: With white and your liner, zig-zag the icing on the gingerbread man. While your black pain is still handy paint his mouth, and dot his "raisin" buttons, and his eyes.

Santa's Beard: Dip your liner into white and then Quaker gray for each stroke of the hair on Santa's beard. Remember to keep the paint watered down for liner work! Start at the bottom of his beard and work your way up overlapping each row of hair. Bring some out on his jacket to make it look real. (Not over his gloves and cuffs though.) The gloves and cuff lay on top of the beard.)

Fur: With a deersfoot or scruffy brush and white, texturize his fur. Not too heavy - just give it some body so it doesn't look too smooth.

Quaker Gray: Shade the beard and mustache as shown in photograph. Shade cuffs and fur on hat.

Holly: With end of paint brush apply berries on the holly.

You are finished painting! Allow to dry overnight. With a piece of gauze, apply neutral past wax. Polish to a soft sheen with a clean piece of gauze.

Assembly Instructions

Sand the areas that will touch each other when glued. This will remove the paint so that the glue will hold properly. Don't forget to sand a small area underneath where the holly is to be glued. (dotted area) Apply yellow wood glue to areas on Santa that touch the wreath, and on holly. Line up Santa's hands with the hole in the wreath, and make sure his head is on straight - not turned to the left or right. Apply pressure until dry.

Cut the ribbon into seven even lengths (9"). Thread a ribbon through the hole in each of the small toys, and tie a knot. Bring the tops of all the ribbons even. Twist and thread through the 1/4" hole in the wreath and Santa's hands. Bring the ribbons up so that all the toys hang at different lengths. Tie a knot.

Now take a ribbon from each of the knot and tie it in a bow. Make two bows. Tie on the bells. Cut any extremely long ribbons to an attractive length. Attach a sawtooth hanger to the back and hang.

Chapter 14

More Neat Projects

More Neat Projects

GRANDCHILDREN WALL HANGING.

See color section for a full color photograph of this completed project.

This is one of my favorite designs. I have six grandchildren, but I allowed for one more just in case! This piece was also cut for me by Newell Hubbard.

Wood: **12″ x 12″ x 1/4″ Baltic birch.**

Blade: **#3 double tooth.**

Table: **Square.**

Additional supplies needed: Seven 1/4″ brass cup hooks. (depending on the size of your family) If the ones you find have a large round base on them, remove it with a pair of pliers.

Before you begin. Since there is a great deal of work in this piece, I recommend you stack at least two together and do two at once. When cutting two increase the blade size to a # 5 blade (reverse tooth to prevent bottom chip out). I would have you use a #3 reverse tooth blade but as far as I know, no one is manufacturing these yet. (If you know of a source for these - let me know!) If you do four at a time increase the blade size to a #6.

SAND WOOD FIRST ! I know that you advanced wood workers are questioning why on earth would anyone sand first? There is a very good reason for this in this case. Since the finished piece is rather fragile, it is a lot less likely to break or get damaged if you sand before the fretwork is done.

Cutting Directions

If you are stack-cutting, end-tape your pieces together

Drill pilot holes as indicated by X's and into those areas that have been blacked out.

Make all the inside cuts first. (refer to inside cutting in Scroll Saw Basics Chapter if you need advice on this.)

Cut straight across the bottom of the piece, detaching the hearts.

Now cut out around the outside edge to complete the pattern.

Lastly, cut the hearts out. You can cut them individually if desired. Better yet, take the piece of wood from the bottom that you cut off and cut in half. End-tape it, apply four of the heart patterns and cut them out.

When finished you will end up with eight small hearts.

I wouldn't recommend painting this. Instead use a liquid stain and seal with a clear finish.

The small hearts may be stained with Delta Crimson Red - thinned down with water 3 -1. Names are applied with liner brush or Sharpie marker.

HONEY POT BANK

See color section for a full color photograph of this completed project.

Two pieces of 6" x 6" x 1/8" ply

One piece of 6" x 6" x 1 3/4" pine

One musical bank slot

Yellow wood glue and clamps

#9 & #3 double tooth blades

Spray glue

Cutting Directions

Make copies of patterns.

First, cut your wood pieces to proper size. Stack them together with the thicker pine piece in the center. Use wide

Teddy on a Swing Patterns
enlarge 33%

WELCOME !!

TOP VIEW

drill here

drill here

TOP VIEW OF SEAT

DRILL

masking tape to secure the outside edges. Apply the pattern for the top and cut with a #9 scroll saw blade. Remove pattern.

Draw line on inside where indicated on pattern and cut that section out. (Save this piece) Glue the top and bottom to the center section and clamp.

While that is drying cut a 3/4″ slice off the top of the piece you cut out of the 1 ¾″ pine. Measure the width, and length of the smallest section of the bank slot movement you have chosen. Draw that exact size and shape on the slice of wood. (Center it!) Next draw a little "slot" down the middle of it. Change the blade to a #3, put a small piece of cardboard over the hole in your table, and tape it in place. Drill a little hole in the center of the slot and cut out that area. Glue that piece into the top of the Honey pot, and clamp until dry. Fill any gaps with wood filler.

When dry, sand entire piece and insert the bank slot. If for some reason the bank slot is too tight, use an emery board and gently sand down the hole until it slips in easily.

Painting Directions

Paint the bear and pot in your choice of color.

Use a Sharpie pen to paint on the details.

Advanced painters may want to enhance this piece with shading, etc. It will be still very cute, however, with a simple paint scheme.

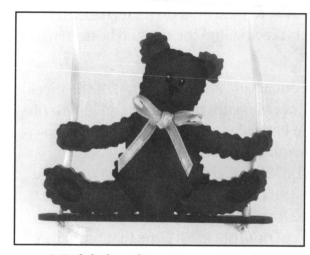

You can really be creative with this design. It was originally designed by my sister Mary in a small version to be worn as a necklace. The swing ropes made the "necklace part". There was no tree in the original version.

My husband came up with the idea of having the bear swinging from a tree, so it became a wall hanging for a child's room. Recently I came up with a "welcome sign" version. I have given you you the full size pattern for the child's room wall hanging here. You can enlarge from this to make a welcome sign if you like.

Special drilling directions for all three designs: When cutting the teddy bear out, start cutting at the tips of his "fingers" on one side, cut up his arm around his head and to the tip of his fingers on his other hand. Stop! Take the piece to the drill press at this time and drill the holes through his hands and legs. There is less danger of pressure breakage doing it this way than if you cut the section between his arms and legs out. After drilling, continue cutting him out.

Necklace: See special drilling directions before cutting. Cut the teddy bear from a piece of 1/4″ birch ply, and the swing seat from a piece of 1/8″ birch ply. Finish according to painting instructions, and when dry thread a 24″ piece of 1/8″ off white ribbon up through the seat, through his foot and hand, back down through the other hand and foot, and finally down through the other side of the seat. Adjust for proper length. Tie a large enough knot under the seat so that the ribbon will not come through the hole. The teddy will swing whenever you bend.

Wall Hanging

Wood:

Teddy Bear:	**6" x5" x1/2" Pine**
Branch:	**12" x 11" x 3/4" Pine.**
Leaves:	**3 pieces of 6" x 1/8" Baltic birch plywood**
Swing seat:	**6" x 3/4" 1/4" pine**
Mounting board:	**12"x 3 "x3/4" pine.**
Swing rope:	**3 ply package twine, available at the grocery store**
Blade:	**# 5 double tooth.**

Sawtooth picture hanger

Copy patterns and apply to appropriate pine pieces with spray glue. Stack the 1/8″ plywood and secure with masking tape. Apply the leaf patterns (Put as many leaves as you can fit onto the top piece) and cut out the leaves. Remember, the number you cut out will be multiplied by three.

Cut teddy bear out. Cut swing seat out, and drill the 1/8″ holes you will need to put the rope through where indicated. Cut branch out. Cut mounting board out . Router all the way around on one side, with router bit of your choice. (I prefer a roman ogee for this particular piece.)

Attach tree to board with 1 ¼″ #6 flat head wood screw. You will need to counter sink these from the back. You may prefer to just put a sawtooth hanger on the back of the branch itself and hand it flat on the wall instead of having it stick out. If so, eliminate the mounting board.

Sand, and Finish according to painting instructions, and when dry attach swing "rope" the same as for the necklace, except you will be using a longer piece of rope, and cutting it in half, so you can tie it around the tree. Glue leaves on with hot glue. There is no set pattern for leaf placement.

Welcome sign: You may want to enlarge the pattern for this. Directions are the same for wall hanging except for the sign which is glued into place (between teddy's hands) after painting is finished.

HEART WALL POCKET

This is another piece that can be enlarged to accomodate a large floral arrangement, or shrunk down small enough to wear as a pin with a very tiny floral arrangment inside. The directions that follow are for the wall pocket.

Wood: **1 piece 8″x 8″x 3/4″ pine.**

            1 piece 8″x 8″x 1/2″ pine

            1 piece 8″x 8″x 1/8″ Baltic Birch

Table: **Square**

Blade: **#5 Reverse tooth**

Cut all pieces to size, and stack them together. Bind with masking tape to hold. Cut out. Remove the masking tape and the bottom section

Stack together the top 1/8″ Baltic Birch, and the center 3/4" piece of pine . Secure with masking tape and cut out on the straight line. Remove tape and the 1/8″ piece.

Cut the 3/4″ piece on the dotted line. Be careful. Do not break this piece.

Put the bow pattern on the remainder of the 1/8″ piece of ply and cut out.

Drill holes in the heart where indicated by arrows.

Cut away the areas marked by an X.

Sand the pieces. Apply yellow wood glue along the bottom edges of the center piece (3/4″ pine). Line this up with the bottom heart piece, and press firmly to distribute glue. Wipe excess glue, and clamp. Check again for glue overflow and wipe away with a damp cloth.

When glue has dried, sand smooth the edges of the heart. Even them up if they do not align perfectly.

Paint with your favorite color of Delta Paints and finish with clear varnish.

After project has dried, arrange flowers inside the pocket and hang.

Thought: For a little girls room I would put two little rag dolls inside with their arms hanging over, and call them her "trouble dolls". Each night when she goes to bed she should tell all her troubles to the dolls, put them under her pillow, and in the morning her troubles will be gone. You will be surprised how little girls can believe in such wonderful "miracles".

EARRING OR RING BOX

See color section for full color photograph of this completed project.

1 piece 6″x 6″x 1 3/4″ Pine

4″x 4″x 1/2″ Pine

1/4″ dowel 1″ long.

Wood glue

7/8″ Forstner bit.

1/4″ drill bit.

#9 and #3 double tooth blades

Make copies of pattern.

Cut wood to size and apply patterns with spray adhesive.

Cut teddy bear out of 1¾" pine using the #9 blade. Be sure to feed square into the wood to make a nice straight cut.

Apply the heart pattern to the thinner wood and cut it out.

Mark dowel hole on the top of the two inch piece, and on the bottom of the 1/4" piece. (Just turn the pattern over, align it on the bottom of the heart, and mark it.) The pine is soft enoughto push firmly with a pencil leaving an indentation.

Drill a 1/4" hole 5/8" deep in the thicker piece. Drill a 1/4" hole 1/4" deep in the thinner pine where marked on the back of the heart. You do not want the drill to pierce the top surface of the heart.

Mark the three holes in the heart of the 1 ¾" wood and drill with a 7/8" Forstner bit. If you do not have a Forstner, you can use any 7/8" bit, the Forstner just leaves a much cleaner hole.

Sand the pieces, and glue the dowel into the "lid". Do not glue it into the base as it will not open if you do.

Sand and seal with Delta's clear wood sealer.

Paint as desired.

TIC TAC TOE TEDDIES

See color section for a full color photograph of this completed project.

Supplies

7½"x 7"x 3/4" Birch

2 pcs. 1½"x 5" maple or other hardwood

2 pcs. dowel 1/4"x1½"

#5, #3 double tooth blades

Make four copies of the teddy bear pattern. Stack the two pieces of maple together, and secure with 1/2" masking tape. Install a #3 blade in your saw. Apply pattern to the wood with

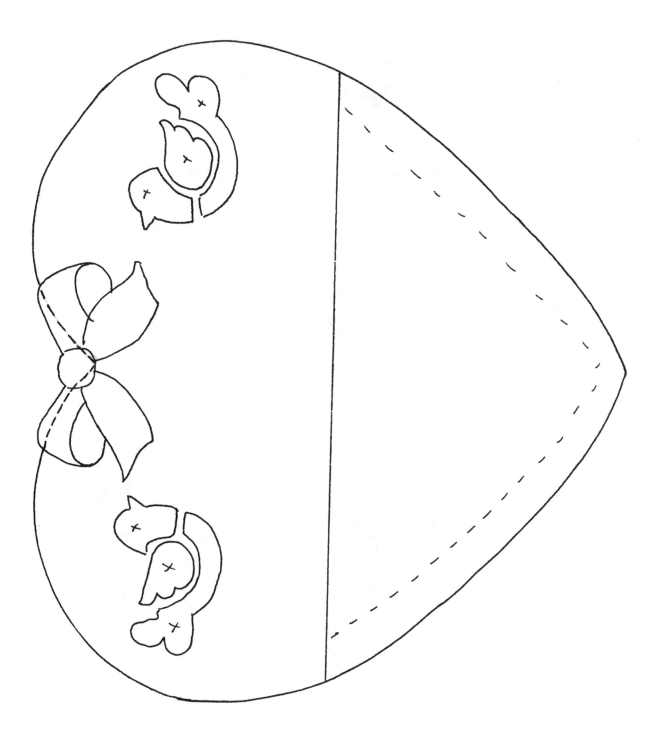

Earring or Ring Box

7/8" holes 5/8" deep

1/4

DRILL HOLE 1/4" x 5/8" deep INSERT 1/4" dowel + glue in.

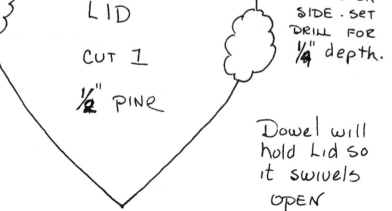

LID

CUT 1

1/2" PINE

1/4

Drill 1/4" hole FROM BACK SIDE. SET DRILL FOR 1/4" depth.

Dowel will hold Lid so it swivels OPEN

spray glue. Drill a 1/4″ hole in their chests for the dowel. Cut them out. By cutting out four of them in this manner, you will end up with eight.

Install the #5 blade. Apply the heart pattern and cut it out.

Drill a 1/4″ hole about 1/2″ deep on each side of the board where the Teddies sit.

Glue in the dowels. Allow to dry.

Sand. Seal with clear wood sealer. When dry, lightly sand again. Tack to remove any dust.

Painting Instructions

Palette. Delta Ceramcoat.

Tomato Spice

Silver

Black

Golden Brown

Autumn Brown

Brushes: **#12 flat** **#5 round** **10/0 Liner**

Trace the pattern, and line it up on the wood. Slip a piece of carbon under it, and with a stylus or pencil trace over the lines with a slight pressure to transfer the pattern to the wood.

You will find using a ruler will be very helpful in making nice straight lines.

With the #12 flat, base area outside squares in TS. Try dampening the area with the #12 flat before applying paint. This helps keep the paint from streaking. Dampen just the area you are going to paint, not the entire piece. In other words, paint with water first.

Base squares in Silver.

With the #5 round, paint half of the bears GB; the other half in AB. As you finish painting each one put the handle of the brush all the way through the hole to remove any paint.

Put a little dolly parton heart on each bear with the stylus and TS.

Dot the eyes and noses in B with your stylus.

Paint the lines on the game board with your liner and thinned Blk. paint. If you do not feel comfortable with a liner, you can use a "Sharpie". Use a ruler that has cork on the back side, otherwise you will find the ink smearing.

When you have finished painting and the project is dry, sand lightly with a piece of crumpled brown paper bag. Finish with a coat of clear varnish.

FINE FISH CUTTING BOARD OR SANDWICH BOARD

See color section for a full color photograph of this project.

Cutting Board

This was designed for the husband of a friend. He is a fisherman and this project is perfect to cut bait on.

Wood:	**Corian Tile 7″ x 10″ by 1″.**
Blade:	**#2 Ultra Blade**

This is easy ! Apply pattern and cut. No sanding no staining - nothing else required. (you may drill a 3/8″ hole about 1/8″ deep into the Corian for the eye if you wish.) Detail is applied with white transfer paper, and then traced over with a black "Sharpie" pen. Wash and use.

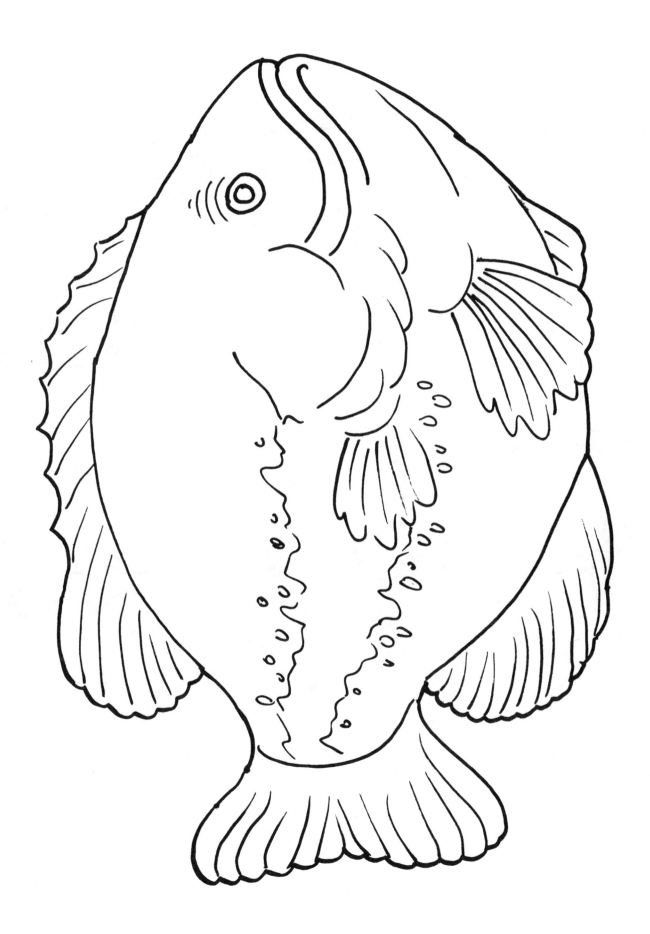

Curtain Tiebacks
enlarge 20%

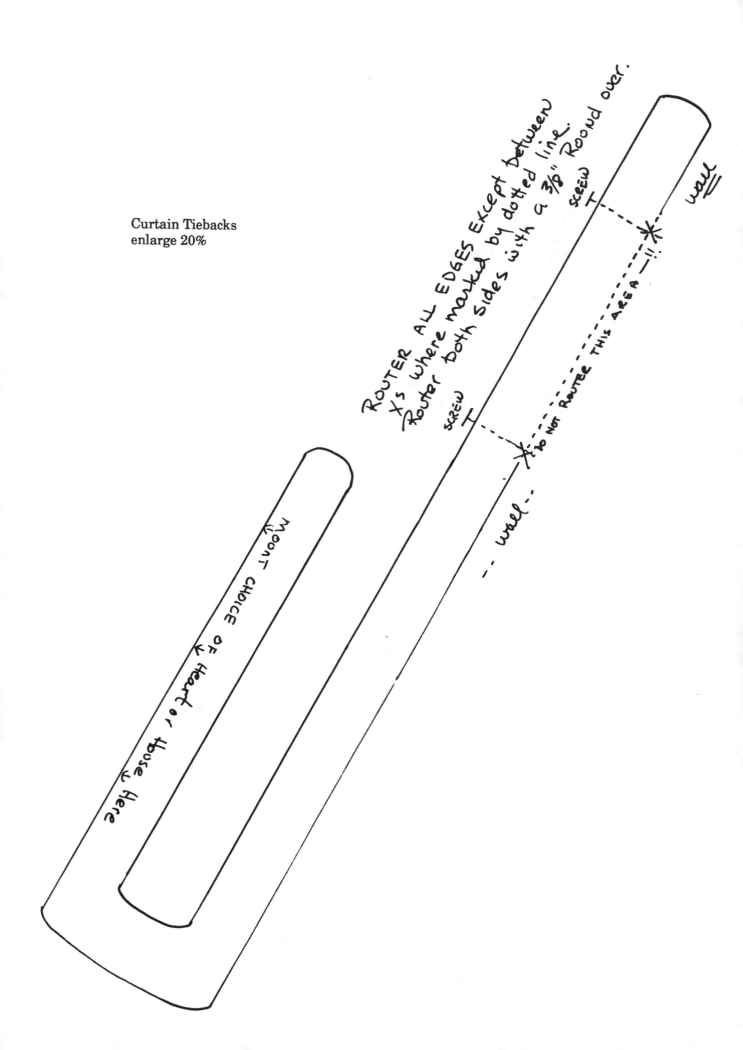

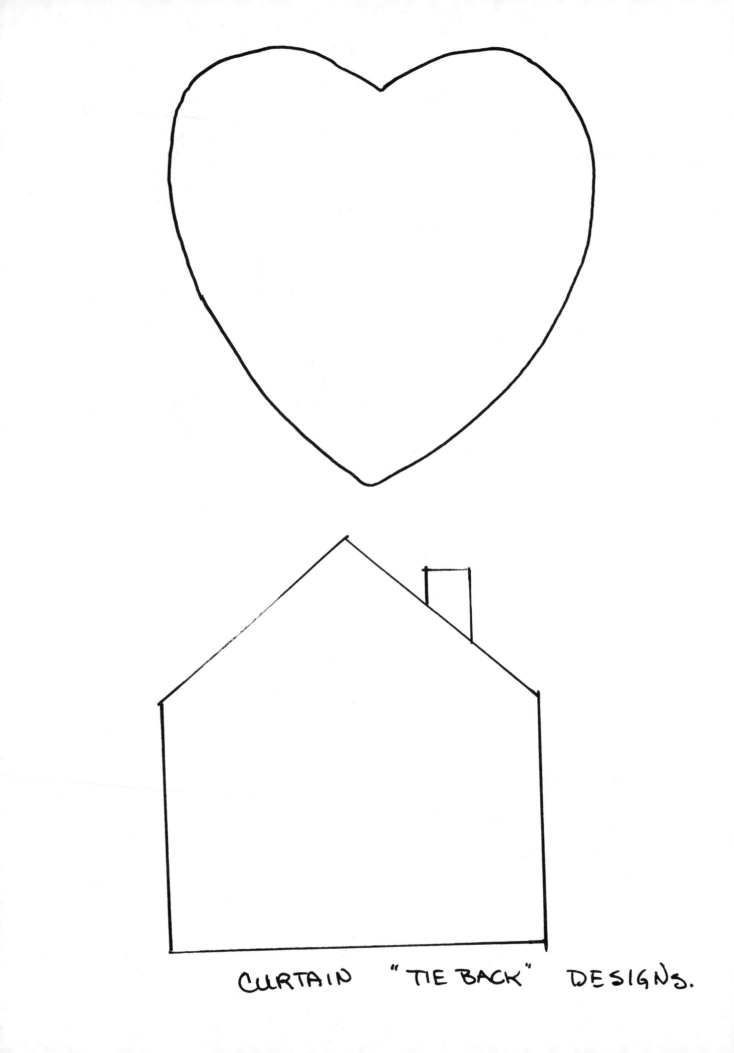

CURTAIN "TIE BACK" DESIGNS.

Sandwich board:

Wood: **7" x 10" x 1" Oak**

Blade: **#9 Double tooth or# 4 Ultra blade.**

Supplies: **One 3/8" oak button plug for eye.**

Same as for Cutting Board except you will want to drill an "eye" hole large enough for the plug.

(Drill a test hole in a piece of scrap wood first to make sure the button will fit snugly.) Then drill hole,and glue button plug in place for eye. Under no circumstances use the "Sharpie" to apply the details. It is toxic ! A sandwich board does not need the details anyway. It takes away from the beauty of the wood grain.

Pour a little oil on the board and rub it in well, Continue until it no longer absorbs. Buff to a nice shine and you are ready for cutting. Wash board with soap and water after each use, and re-season with one coat of oil. (like old cast iron pots!)

CURTAIN "TIE BACKS"

There are two different "front " patterns for these included.
The directions are the same for both.

Wood:	**13" x 3" x 1" oak or other hardwood that will fit your particular decor.**
	5 1/2" x 5 1/2" x 1" pine
Blade:	**#9 double tooth or # 4 Ultra Blade.**
Supplies:	**Four 2 1/2" #8 round head wood screws per set.**

Apply Pattern A to the hardwood piece with spray glue. Cut out.. Drill mounting holes where indicated. Router a 3/8" round over on both sides from x mark to x mark. THIS AREA MUST BE LEFT FLAT ON THE SIDE THAT IS TO BE AGAINST THE WALL.

Apply design you have chosen to the pine piece and cut out. I used a 3/8" roundover on the heart to soften it. This is optional.

Sand both pieces. I left the oak natural, and just waxed it with paste wax.

The Heart is painted with Delta's Copen Blue, and waxed with clear paste wax for the "country look".

Suggestion: - if you have decorated with wallpaper, and want to continue the theme. Take a pattern off the wall paper, enlarge it to the appropriate size, paint it, and use it for the top piece. If you have a design that is already large enough, you can even glue the design right on the wood, cut it out and mount it. No painting necessary!

ELEPHANT LEAVE A NOTE

They say an elephant never forgets, but I don't know about this guy. He looks like he is trying to remember what he already forgot. But if you will write down all the little things you don't want to forget, he promises to "remember" them for you.

Wood:	10"x 1"x 1" pine
Blade:	#3 double tooth.
Table:	Square.

Copy pattern and apply to wood piece. Cut around the outside pattern line.

Sand, seal and paint if desired. Directions follow for painting.

After you have applied your choice of finish, put a piece of double sticky tape on the back of a 3 x 5 tablet and place on the elephants back as indicated on pattern.

Special instructions: For those of you who would like a bit more of a challenge, you may want to put a routered edge around this piece. Be very careful around the tail if you do !.

Painting Instructions

Palette: Delta Ceramcoat

Black

Ivory

Nimbus Gray

Gypsy Rose

White

Brushes:	#12 Flat #5 round #10/0 liner
	two 2" foam brushes

Seal with clear wood sealer, using a foam brush. When dry, sand and tack to remove any residue.

With your other foam brush, base coat the entire elephant (Except for the hole in his trunk) with Nimbus Gray. Base the hole in the trunk in Gypsy Rose.

With the #5 round, paint his entire eye area in White. When the White has dried, paint the pupil in Black.

With the #12 flat, and Black , Float all the way around the outside edge. Float in between his legs to indicate that he really has two legs on each end. Float the wrinkles in his skin with black also.

Float around the second line on his ears with black. Float his little toes in black also.

His tusks are painted with your #5 and Ivory. Finally with a 10/0 liner, paint his eyebrows, and outline his eyes.

When he is dry, lightly sand him with a crumpled brown paper bag. Tack, and apply clear varnish.

Put a piece of double sticky tape on the back of the 3x5 notepad and attach to his back.

Chapter 15

Scroll Saw Pattern Treasury

Scroll Saw Pattern Treasury

The following pages contain dozens of new patterns plus some variations on project patterns found elsewhere in this book.

No directions are given.

Let your imagination run wild.

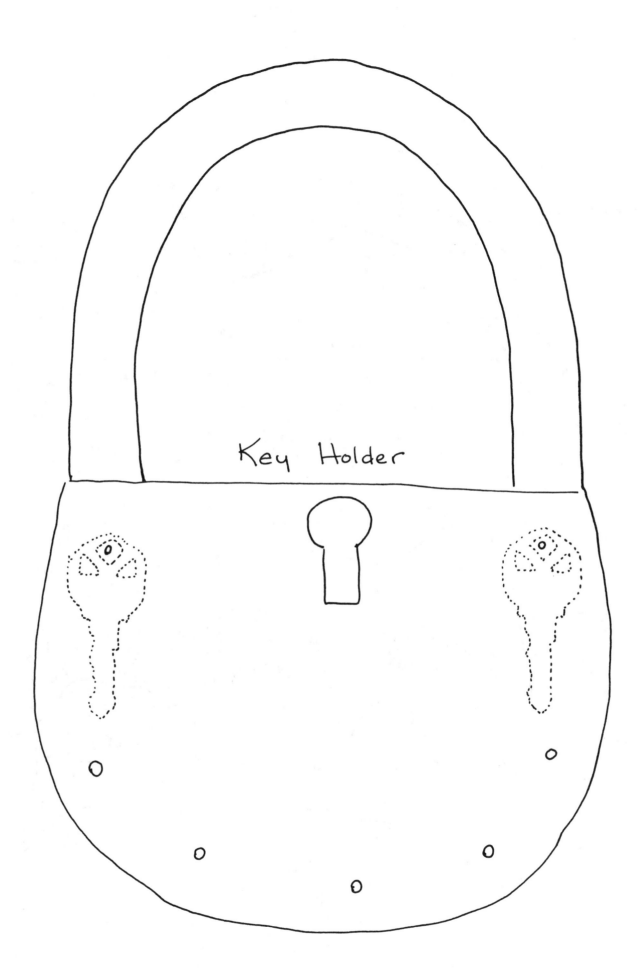

Key Holder

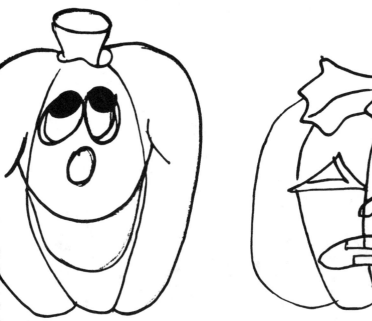

Halloween

Autumn

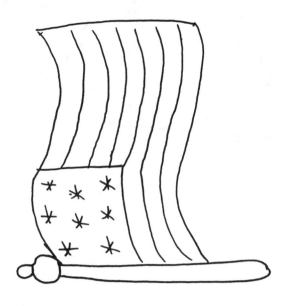

SPORTS

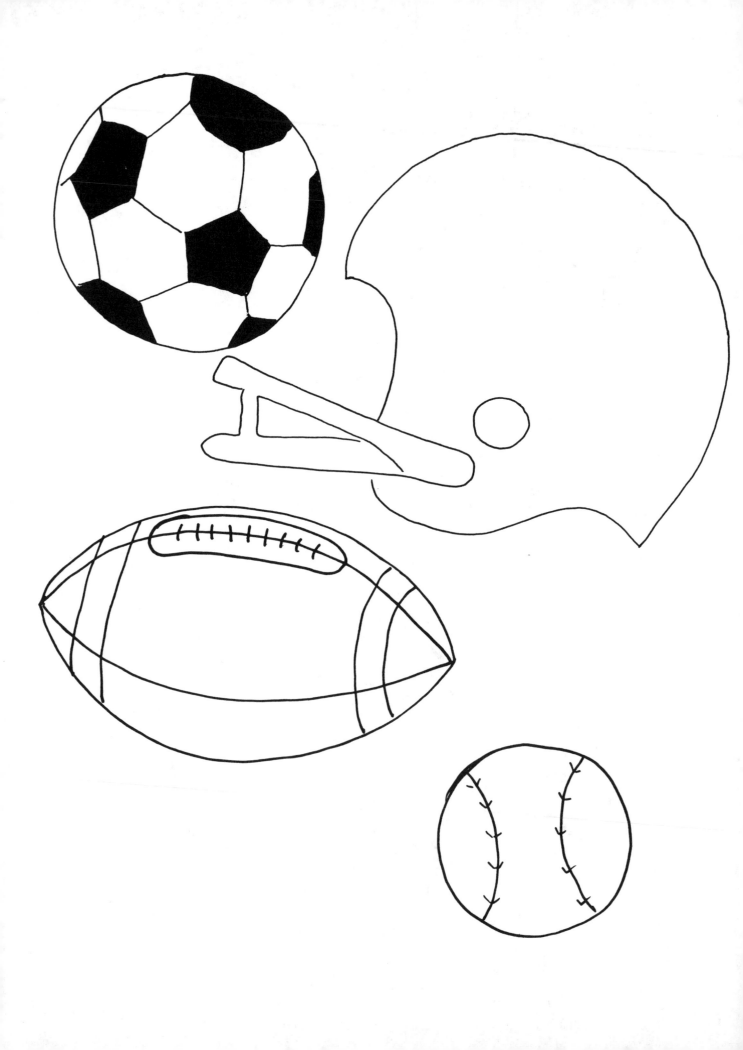

INLAY Patterns

GLOSSARY

Blade Clamp: These are the little pieces that hold the blade in the machine. There are many different types, and styles.

Bottom chip out: When the blade or saw causes the bottom of your wood to chip at the cutting line. Larger blades will cause this more noticeably than the small blades.

Clockwise: To cut in the direction clock hands move in (to the right).

Counter clockwise: To cut in the opposite direction that clock hands move (to the left).

Double tooth blade: These blades have two teeth followed by a space, all the way down the blade. Some have reverse teeth.

Ferrule: Referring to a painters brush, this is the metal part that holds the bristles in.

Fret work or inside cuts: Removing pieces of wood from the center of a piece without cutting into it from the edge.

Multiple cuts: Cutting more than one layer of wood at a time also known as stack-cutting.

Overlay: A special piece of wood or cardboard that is temporarily placed on the scroll saw table to enable you to cut very tiny pieces.

Palette paper: A waxed paper painters use to blend the paint into the brush.

Pivot point: Placing a finger along side or behind the blade at a safe distance, enabling you to turn the wood around smoothly and accurately.

Protractor: A gauge, generally found under the scroll saw table, that tells you the degree of tilt on your table.

Reverse tooth blade: Has 4 or 5 teeth at the bottom that point upwards to come back up through the bottom of the wood to get rid of bottom chip out.

Sealer: A liquid used to seal the wood to avoid warpage, and absorption of too much paint.

Spray glue: Referring to a good repositionable glue in an aerosol can.

Square into the blade: Pushing the wood straight into the blade, and not off to the left or right. This is especially critical when doing puzzles.

Square: In this book it is referring to a small machined metal hobbyist square. It is used to true the blade so that all cuts are made perpendicular.

Stylus: Used in decorative painting to make small dots.

Tack Cloth: A sticky gauze type cloth used to remove saw-dust and lint.

Tension Knob: Generally found in the rear section of the machine on top of the arm. It is usually a knob, and is used to loosen, or tighten the amount of tension on the blade.

Throat: Referring to the distance between the blade on a scroll saw and the back of the "arm". This can vary — from around 14" all the way up to 25 inches.

Tracing paper: A thin translucent paper you can see through.

Transfer or Graphite paper: Used to apply pattern to wood, Corian, etc.

Ultra Blades: A new type of blade that cuts very aggressively! The configuration of the teeth is almost straight out, rather than the traditional downward position.

Variable speed switch: A switch or dial that allows you to vary your scroll saw speed usually in the range from 200 strokes per minute to 2000 strokes per minute (spm).

SOURCES

COMPANY	SOURCE FOR:
Joanne Lockwood *3 Bears Workshop* 7806 Antelope Road Citrus Heights, CA 95610 SASE please when writin with questions Brochure $2.00	Hegner Scrollsaws All related items for scroll saw users woodcrafters Decorative painting supplies Books, Pattern packets, and supplies. Brass hardware for necklaces & lockets (916) 726-7063 Fax (916) 726-9348
Advanced Machinery *Imports* AMI Ltd. P.O. Box 312 New Castle, DE 19720 Catalogue available	Hegner Saws & supplies Blades—Books Other quality machinery. (302) 322-2226
The Berry Basket P.O. Box 925 Centralia, WA 98531 Catalog available	Folding Trivet / Basket patterns & Books (206) 736-7020
Country Sunshine Kathie Rueger 7516 E Mulberry Evansville, IN 47715	Patterns, pattern packets and books. (812) 476-5720
Delta /Shiva Corp. 2550 Pellissier Place. Whittier CA 90601.	Delta paints and products used in this book. They sell though distributors only. Call if you cannot find a distribu- tor . They will tell you where to find one. (800) 423-4135

Jackie Shaw Studio Inc.
Rt. 3, Box 155
Smithsburg MD 21783

Brush stroke work book
Jackie has four books in
this series, and you will
want them all! Videos
also available.

**Lanis Wholesale &
Craft Supply**
11367 Trade Center Drive
Suite 110
Rancho Cordova, CA

Everything the Decorative
painter needs. Brushes,
paints, palettes, graphite
paper, Books, wood pieces,
findings, turnings etc.
Friendly service, with a wide
variety of supplies
(916) 852-7468

Loew Cornell Inc.
573 Chestnut Ave.
Teaneck NJ 07666-8810

Brushes - wholesale to distrib-
utors only. They will refer you
to suppliers and teachers.

Penn State Machinery
2850 Comly Rd.
Philadelphia PA 19154
Catalog available

Scroll saws and other machinery and accessories.

Quality WoodCrafters
P.O. Box 19374
Raleigh, NC 27619

Wooden toys and more.

Seyco Sales
1414 Cranford Drive
Garland Texas, 75041

Excalibur Scroll Saws
Blades, and Templates
Books and Patterns

BRING YOUR WOOD CUTOUTS TO LIFE!

Our books can help you give each of your scroll saw projects a unique personality and professional finishing touch—with just the right style of decorative painting.

Use our *basic technique and reference* books to learn to do your own decorative design and painting. These books are meant to teach **you** everything you need to know about color mixing, shading, blending, highlighting, brush strokes, finishing techniques and much, much more. **You'll soon be decorating your pieces in a style that is uniquely yours,** using colors and designs that you know will go just right with your project.

Use our *pattern and instruction* books as sources for popular designs with plenty of personality built right in. These books feature full size line drawings for projects you can cut on your scroll saw and thorough, step-by-step painting instructions, ranging from the very easy to the downright challenging. You'll find every design idea you could imagine and many you'd never have dreamed of. Big, full-color photos show you all painting details.

And if you like to learn while watching, we have a selection of *videos* ranging from basic brush stroke techniques to step-by-step painting of specific projects. See our catalog for complete descriptions of contents.

Send $1.00 for our color catalog with descriptions of our over 100 titles.

Order direct and receive 15% discount. You may also order directly from among the books shown on these pages. You may charge your order to VISA, Mastercard, or American Express or send a check or money order. Simply list the books you want, total their cost and add 2.50 for postage. Mention "Woodcutters' Special" on your first order and deduct 15%.

Address: Jackie Shaw Studio, Inc., 13306 Edgemont Rd., Smithsburg, MD 21783.

BASIC TECHNIQUES AND REFERENCES

FUN-damentals of Freehanding is a four-part series of painting instruction books designed by Jackie Shaw to enable the painter to gain mastery of brush strokes and freehanding techniques through carefully planned, progressive instruction.

Each numbered part of the series is a separate, self-contained book focusing on specific subjects. The series was developed especially for classroom use and for individual self-study.

Part 1—#39 Jackie's Brush Stroke Workbook. Features 11 basic brush strokes and three brush stroke exercises. Learn to master the liner, flat, and round brushes. Included is a bonus sheet of Magic Paper which can be repeatedly used for brush stroke practice by painting with water. 24 pages. Acrylics **$6.95**

Part 1—#40 Beginner's Guide to Freehand Decorative Painting. This definitive text includes thorough instructions for color mixing theory, creating color schemes, surface preparation and finishing for wood and tin, antiquing, basic brush strokes, combining strokes for creating decorative designs, proper brush loading techniques, and interesting backgrounds. 64 pages, including 52 in color. Acrylics **$8.95**

Part 3—#9 Freehanding with Jackie. Acclaimed as a classic! Contains over 200 border designs, from simple to complex, and a wealth of information on brush stroke and liner techniques. Offers confidence building aids to help you paint more freely and imaginatively. 48 pages. Acrylics **$6.95**

Part 4—#24 Jackie's Freehanding Seminar, Book 1. This immensely popular book, based on Jackie's seminars at her Old Stone Mill studio, is designed to help the painter develop creative and imaginative designs from basic brush strokes. It also provides full instructions on additional strokes to add further to the painter's skills. 48 pages, including 43 in color. Acrylics **$8.95**

#5 There's A Rainbow In My Paintbox by Jackie Shaw. Mix endless colors and tints from red, yellow, and blue plus black and white. Learn to build color schemes, work with color values and temperatures and, most importantly, understand what you do. 28 pages, including 10 in color. Oils/Acrylics **$5.95**

#57 Creative Painting by Jackie Shaw. In her most thorough and colorful book yet, Jackie provides an eye opening tour of marvelous ways in which decorative painting can be put to use for home decor, clothing, gifts, and fun. Written as a companion to Jackie's Creative Painting television show, this book stands by itself as a most comprehensive primer of decorative painting. 80 pages, including 74 in color. Acrylics **$9.95**

#65 Acrylic & Fabric Painter's Reference Book by Susan Bentley. This book reflects the author's determination to produce the most complete and thoroughly researched reference book possible.   Chapters provide detailed information on supplies; surface preparation and finishing; transferring patterns; brush strokes; painting techniques; the many facets of the decorative painting community. Includes 61 pages of charts of independently researched and cross-referenced color conversions between eight major paint brands, as well as a thorough glossary and index. 184 pages. Acrylics **$12.95**

#84 The Index of Decorative Painting. A 4-part, cross-referenced listing of decorative painting books, authors, patterns, publishers. Using information provided by over 200 authors, nine thousand patterns from 800 books are listed by topic. At a glance anyone can learn what is available in decorative painting ideas. Answer questions such as: what

books have "bears" in them? What patterns are in a book named "Jackie's Golden Goose"? What books are available from author "X"? 140 pages. **$9.95**

PATTERN AND INSTRUCTION BOOKS

The projects in each book are shown on its front cover. See our catalog for descriptions of the contents.

#19 $4.95   #27 $6.95   #52 $6.95   #62 $6.95   #86 $6.95

#25 $6.50   #29 $7.50   #26 $6.95   #30 $6.95   #36 $6.95

#41 $6.95   #47 $6.95   #54 $6.95   #60 $6.95   #67 $6.95

#81 $5.95   #23 $6.50   #45 $6.95   #48 $6.95   #53 $5.95

#46 $6.95   #51 $6.95   #71 $6.95   #73 #7.50   #89 $7.50

#95 $8.95   #90 $5.95   #76 $7.50   #63 $7.95   #61 $6.95

#80 $5.95   #74 $7.50   #88 $8.95

jackie shaw studio

13306 Edgemont Road
Smithsburg, MD 21783

Take a Look at Our Other Fine Woodworking Books

Woodcarving Books by George Lehman
Learn new techniques as you carve these projects designed by professional artists and carver George Lehman. These best-selling books by a master carver are invaluable reference books, PLUS each book contains over 20 ready-to-use patterns.

Book One - **Carving Realistic Game and Songbirds - Patterns and instructions**
Enthusiastically received by carvers across the US and Canada. George pays particular attention to the needs of beginning carvers in this volume. 20 patterns, over 70 photos, sketches and reference drawing.
ISBN# 1-56523-004-3   96 pages, spiral bound, 14 x 11 inches, includes index, resources $19.95

Book Two - **Realism in Wood - 22 projects, detailed patterns and instructions**
This volume features a selection of patterns for shorebirds and birds of prey in addition to all-new duck and songbird patterns. Special sections on adding detail, burning.
ISBN# 1-56523-005-1,   112 pages, spiral bound, 14 x 11 inches, includes index, resources $19.95

Book Three - **Nature in Wood - patterns for carving 21 smaller birds and 8 wild animals**
Focuses on songbirds and small game birds . Numerous tips and techniques throughout including instruction on necessary skills for creating downy feather details and realistic wings. Wonderful section on wild animal carvings with measured patterns.
ISBN #1-56523-006-X   128 pages, soft bound, 11 x 8.5 inches, includes index, resources $16.95

Book Four - **Carving Wildlife in Wood- 20 Exciting Projects**
Here is George's newest book for decorative woodcarvers with never-before-published patterns. Tremendously detailed, these patterns appeal to carvers at all skill levels. Patterns for birds of prey, ducks, wild turkey, shorebirds and more! Great addition to any carvers library - will be used again and again.
ISBN #1-56523-007-8   96 pages, spiral-bound, 14 x 11 inches, includes index, resources $19.95

Easy to Make Wooden Inlay Projects: Intarsia   *by Judy Gale Roberts*
Intarsia is a method of making picture mosaics in wood, using a combination of wood grains and colors. The techniques and step-by-step instructions in this book will have you completing your own beautiful pieces in short order. Written by acknowledged expert Judy Gale Roberts, who has her own studio and publishes the Intarsia Times newsletter, produces videos, gives seminars and writes articles on the Intarsia method. Each project is featured in full color and this well written, heavily illustrated features over 100 photographs and includes index and directory of suppliers
ISBN# 56523-023-X   250 pages, soft cover, 8.5 x 11 inches $19.95

Two more great scroll saw books by Judy Gale Roberts! Scroll Saw Fretwork Patterns
Especially designed for the scroll saw enthusiast who wishes to excel, the 'fine line design' method helps you to control drift error found with thick line patterns. Each book features great designs, expert tips, and patterns on oversized (up to 11" x 17"!) sheets in a special "lay flat" spiral binding. Choose the original Design Book 1 with animal and fun designs, or Design Book Two featuring "Western- Southwestern" designs.
Scroll Saw Fretwork Pattern, Design Book One "The Original" $14.95
Scroll Saw Fretwork Patterns, Design Book Two "Western-Southwestern" $16.95

Scroll Saw Woodcrafting Magic! Complete Pattern and How-to Manual   *by Joanne Lockwood*
Includes complete patterns drawn to scale. You will be amazed at how easy it is to make these beautiful projects when you follow Joanne's helpful tips and work from these clear, precise patterns. Never-before-published patterns for original and creative toys, jewelry, and gifts. Never used a scroll saw? The tutorials in this book will get you started quickly. Experienced scroll-sawers will delight in these all-new, unique projects, perfect for craft sales and gift-giving. Written by Joanne Lockwood, owner of Three Bears Studio in California and the president of the Sacramento Area Woodworkers; she is frequently featured in national woodwork and craft magazines.
ISBN# 1-56523-024-8   180 pages, soft cover, 8.5 x 11 inches $14.95

Making Signs in Wood with Your Router   *by Paul Merrills*
I f you own a router, you can produce beautiful personalized signs and designs easily and inexpensively. This is the complete manual for beginners and professionals. Features over 100 clear photos, easy-to-follow instructions, ready-to-use designs, and six complete sign making alphabets. Techniques range from small nameplates to world-class showpieces trimmed with gold leaf.
ISBN# 56523-026-4 250 pages, 8.5 x 11 inches; includes index and suppliers directory $19.95

To order: If you can't find these at your favorite bookseller you may order direct from the publisher at the prices listed above plus $2.00 per book shipping.
Send check or money order to:

Fox Chapel Publishing
Box 7948D
Lancaster, Pennsylvania , 17604